C000059632

A SHORT GUIDE TO OPERATIONAL RISK

SHORT GUIDES TO RISK SERIES

Risk is a far more complex and demanding issue than it was ten years ago. Risk managers may have expertise in the general aspects of risk management and in the specifics that relate directly to their business, but they are much less likely to understand other more specialist risks. Equally, Company Directors may find themselves falling down in their duty to manage risk because they don't have enough knowledge to be able to talk to their risk team in a sensible way.

The short guides to risk are not going to make either of these groups experts in the subject but will give them plenty to get started and in a format and an extent (circa 100 pages) that is readily digested.

Titles in the series will include:

- Climate Risk
- Compliance Risk
- Employee Risk
- Environmental Risk
- Fraud Risk
- Information Risk
- Intellectual Property Risk
- Kidnap and Ransom Risk
- Operational Risk
- Purchasing Risk
- Reputation Risk
- Strategic Risk
- Supply Chain Risk
- Tax Risk
- Terrorism Risk

For further information, visit www.gowerpublishing.com/ shortguidestorisk

A Short Guide to Operational Risk

David Tattam

GOWER

Published by
Gower Publishing Limited
Wey Court East
Union Road
Farnham, Surrey
GU9 7PT England

Gower Publishing Company
110 Cherry Street
Suite 3-1
Burlington, VT 05401-3818
USA

www.gowerpublishing.com

British Library Cataloguing in Publication Data
Tattam, David.
A short guide to operational risk. -- (Short guides to
business risk series)
1. Operational risk. 2. Risk management.
I. Title II. Series
658.1'55-dc22

ISBN: 978-0-566-09183-4 (hbk)
ISBN: 978-1-4094-2891-6 (ebk)

Library of Congress Cataloging-in-Publication Data
Tattam, David.
A short guide to operational risk / David Tattam.
    p. cm. -- (Short guides to business risk)
Includes index.
ISBN 978-0-566-09183-4 (hardback) -- ISBN 978-1-4094-2891-6
(ebook) 1. Risk management. 2. Operational risk. I. Title.
HD61.T38 2011
658.15'5--dc22

2010053763

Printed and bound in Great Britain by the
MPG Books Group, UK

Contents

List of Figures

List of Tables

List of Abbreviations

BAU	Business As Usual
cctv	Closed circuit television
CRO	Chief Risk Officer
CSF	Critical Success Factors
DRP	Disaster Recovery Plan
ERM	Enterprise Risk Management
GOR	Group Operational Risk
IT	Information Technology
KRI	Key Risk Indicator
ORC	Operational Risk Committee
ORM	Operational Risk Management
RAR	Risk Adjusted Return
RCSA	Risk and Control Self Assessment
RORAC	Return On Risk Adjusted Capital
RAROC	Risk Adjusted Return on Capital

Acknowledgements

This book is a culmination of a long journey that started for me in 1983 as an auditor in the UK. Much of the content is as a result of the many experiences I have had over the last 27 years, the many people I have worked with, the many people I have bounced ideas off and the many people, who through their own interest and efforts, have supported my passion in operational risk management. The list is too long to mention but a few special thanks are due.

I would like to thank Martin Samociuk who first encouraged me to take on the challenge of this book and the individuals, particularly Stephanie Brooks, Glen Laslett and my wife Julie for their efforts in reviewing the drafts to turn them into readable quality. To the literally hundreds of training course participants globally that I have had the privilege to train and through their candid comments and ideas have helped mould my risk management views. Also a huge thanks to my family who had to learn not to 'disturb dad' while the book was coming to fruition.

A special thanks to my colleagues at Protecht Advisory where I have been privileged to be able to put many of my ideas into practice through seeing an operational risk system come to life and be implemented at a wide range of clients. And to those clients who have embraced operational risk management and provided invaluable feedback so that we can continue to develop the exciting world of operational risk to a mature discipline that, I truly believe, will gain its rightful place as an essential and critical component of business into the twenty-first century.

All of these have made this book possible.

David Tattam
April 2011

About the Author

David Tattam is a director of Protecht Advisory in Australia, a specialist provider of software, education and consulting services in the risk management field. David founded the company in 1999 after a career which commenced in 1983 in the UK with Grant Thornton International chartered accountants. After qualifying as an ACA in 1985, David emigrated to Australia in 1987 with PwC where he worked in the audit and technical departments. He joined the Industrial Bank of Japan in Australia (now Mizuho Corporate Bank) as Head of Operations before establishing the middle office risk management group and becoming the Head of Risk Management. In 1996 he joined WestLB Bank in Australia as Head of Operations and Risk Management where he remained until 1999.

Throughout his career David has been passionate in developing and delivering risk management training which has seen him deliver risk related courses in over 30 countries across the globe.

Protecht Advisory has provided an outlet for David's passion for all things risk which over the past 11 years has led to the development of Protecht's proprietary enterprise risk management software WORMS®, which has currently been implemented in over 30 clients, a proprietary asset and liability risk management system ALARMS® as well as a comprehensive suite of face-to-face and on-line risk management training. Protecht also provides risk consulting services from methodology development and assurance, through policy development and systems implementation to the facilitation of risk workshops through its team of experienced practitioners.

More information can be found at www.protecht.com.au and David can be contacted on david.tattam@protecht.net.

Foreword

by Jan Schreuder and Alfredo Martinez

'You only find out who is swimming naked when the tide goes out.'

Warren Buffett, Chairman's letter to shareholders 2001, Berkshire Hathaway Inc

These famous words by Warren Buffett describe what many organisations have experienced in the last few years. When the global financial crisis started to bite after years of economic growth and ever increasing corporate profits, organisations suddenly had to place increasing scrutiny on every aspect of their cost base and re-assess the levels of risk running through their operations. To their surprise many found not just opportunities to reduce costs, but their spotlight suddenly revealed many areas of weak control, fraud, non-compliance and operational losses that have been going on for many years and had been considered within acceptable tolerance levels.

In that same period, we have seen a step change in the maturity of operational risk management practices. Some of it has been driven by regulatory changes but most has been the result of an increased level of awareness and expectations of boards and audit and risk committees. Over the last ten years the discipline of operational risk management has grown from fragmented and siloed sets of management practices across a range of risk areas such as security, environment, health and safety, to a well recognised management discipline with a well established terminology, frameworks and practices.

Many lessons have been learned from the operational failures highlighted in the aftermath of the global financial crisis. This provides an opportunity to further improve the way organisations manage and control operational risks. We expect that operational risk management will continue to mature, with much more focus on managing the risks that matter, rather than just spending time on getting the process right. There has probably been no better time to be an operational risk professional.

Historically the focus of operational risk management within the financial services industry has been largely or solely on protecting shareholders from the risk of loss of their capital through preventing bad things from happening. Outside financial services, the focus has been largely on protecting employees' safety in the conduct of their day-to-day duties and maintaining day-to-day operations. Today operational risk managers are taking a much more holistic approach. The role of risk management is seen not just as preventing downside, but also ensuring that opportunities (both present and emerging) for upside are identified and realised. Risk managers are also devoting more time to understanding the impact of business and product decisions on a much wider range of stakeholders such as customers, suppliers, employees, governments and regulators when assessing risks which could impact on the sustainability of the organisation and its 'licence to operate'.

The future of operational risk is equally as exciting and dynamic as its recent past. We are seeing increased focus on setting and reporting risk appetite, identifying and analysing predictive key risk indicators, the quantification of risk and the assessment and measurement of the effectiveness of controls, the use of more sophisticated techniques for root cause analysis, and increased use of scenario analysis to model and simulate the impact of non-routine or irregular events. Alongside the increased quantification of operational risk there is an increasing emphasis on understanding and improving the operational risk culture within organisations and ensuring that it is not eroded by too great a focus on quantification and measurement.

The increased use of the internet for business-to-business and business-to-consumer transactions has meant that the effectiveness and efficiency of organisational processes are much more transparent to customers, suppliers and even regulators, and the failure of a business process is visible immediately to everyone outside and inside the organisation. Leading organisations are starting to apply techniques such as Six Sigma and other process engineering disciplines to make operational risk management more efficient and embed it into core organisational processes. The objective is to build value adding, robust, repeatable and scalable processes that deliver predictable outcomes for customers, suppliers as well as for the organisation itself.

A comprehensive guide to operational risk management could not have come at a better time. Regardless of your industry, managers everywhere are looking to improve the way they identify, assess and manage their operational risks.

This book provides an overview of the concepts and practice of operational management as a guide for anyone from the new graduate to the experienced manager.

Jan Schreuder and Alfredo Martinez
Sydney, April 2011

Jan Schreuder is a partner in the Risk & Controls Solutions practice in PricewaterhouseCoopers. He has been a partner for more than 20 years during most of which he has specialised in operational and technology risk management. Through his career he has advised many clients across multiple industries ranging from banks, insurance companies, utilities, airlines and public sector organisations.

Alfredo Martinez is a director in the Risk & Controls Solutions practice in PricewaterhouseCoopers. He has been a risk and control practitioner for over 13 years specialising in the financial services industry. Throughout his career, which has included time in Sydney, London and Singapore, he has advised many clients on operational and technology risk management opportunities and challenges.

PART 1

Understanding Operational Risk

① What is Operational Risk?

Operational Risk simply comes from doing things, or 'operating'. We all face some degree of operational risk as we all 'do things'. The nature, extent and size of that operational risk is dependent on the nature and extent of our choices as to what we do. The range of actual and potential activities undertaken by humans and organisations is vast, resulting in the related operational risk being equally as extensive.

This book is focused on providing the reader with an in-depth understanding of the nature of operational risk, primarily as it relates to an organisation. It then takes the reader through the processes of identifying, assessing, quantifying and managing operational risk. The practical aspects of how these steps can be applied to an organisation using a range of management tools is then addressed.

Operational risk is but one segment of the total risk that an organisation may encounter, so before the intricacies of operational risk are discussed, the term 'Risk' and its components will be explained together with how they link to operational risk.

RISK

Risk can be described and defined in many ways, including:

- a situation involving exposure to danger

- the possibility that something unpleasant will happen

- the chance of winning

- being exposed to the effects of something that could potentially happen in the future.

The ISO 31000: 2009 *Risk Management – Principles and Guidelines* standard defines risk quite simply as:

> *The effect of uncertainty on objectives*

There are five key features of risk. These are:

Future Potential Event: Risk relates to the potential occurrence of a future event(s), not a past event that has already occurred, although the past may be used to better understand and predict the future.

> *Example, a ski resort is exposed to future changes in weather, specifically snowfall and temperature. Past changes in weather do not pose a risk as these events have already occurred.*

Uncertainty: The potential future event may or may not have uncertainty over whether it will occur or not. For example, over the next ten years, one of the organisation's buildings may or may not catch fire whereas it is almost certain that we will be sick over that same period. In the latter case, where the occurrence of the event is certain, or almost certain, there must be uncertainty over the level of consequence that will result from the event occurring in order for it to be considered a risk. Although sickness may be almost certain, the severity of the sickness is not. Therefore, in order to be a risk, there must be a degree of uncertainty over the occurrence of a specific outcome-consequence. Uncertainty is sometimes referred to as 'likelihood', 'chance', 'probability' or 'frequency'.

> *Example: The occurrence of future snowfalls and their size is uncertain and therefore poses a risk to the ski resort in relation to the risk of not being able to ski. The occurrence of darkness occurring overnight, preventing skiers using the slopes, does not pose a risk, as it is certain.*

The degree of likelihood, amongst other things, is dependent on the length of the future time period over which the risk is being considered. The longer the future time period, the greater the likelihood of the risk occurring within that period.

Impact: To be considered a risk, the future event(s) must have a potential impact on the organisation or person. This potential impact will include a negative aspect (threat) but may also include a positive impact (opportunity). Impact is also sometimes referred to as 'consequence', 'effect' or 'severity'. There are a range of potential consequences and these may differ between types of risk. A consequence may be financial, such as a monetary loss, or non-financial (qualitative), such as damaged reputation. Consequence is the degree of deviation away from the organisation's or person's expected state. The expected state is usually referred to as *'objectives'*. This deviation represents the consequence, which may be positive or negative.

> *Example: The lack of future snowfalls will have a negative consequence on the ski resort as less skiers will take to the slopes and revenue will fall. It is therefore considered a risk.*

Exposure: If the potential future event would, or could, have a consequence on the organisation or person, that organisation or person is said to be '*exposed*' to that risk. The implies that in order to be an 'exposure', the likelihood and the consequence of the risk must be greater than zero. Where a risk has a potential consequence but has no chance of occurring, there is no exposure. Equally, where the potential event is likely but the consequence is zero, there is also no exposure. Risks that create no exposure to one entity may cause an exposure to another entity.

> *Example: Weather risk in the locality of a ski resort in Australia causes a risk exposure to that resort but not to a resort in Canada.*

Intangible: On the one hand risk is intangible in that it is not directly visible. It is like the wind which, although unseen, can result in very visible effects. Likewise, risk, although unseen, can have very visible consequences. On the other hand, the sources of risk such as exposed chemicals, often referred to as 'hazards', are usually very visible.

Risk, although intangible, can be illustrated using a simple diagram. This diagram, known as a probability distribution, uses the above elements (see Figure 1.1).

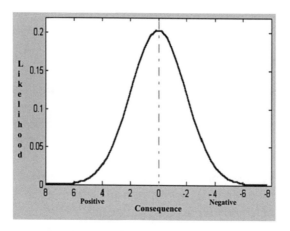

Figure 1.1   Probability distribution

To illustrate, consider the risk of snowfall to the ski resort. The risk of snowfall occurring or not occurring, and to what depth, can lead to a wide range of financial consequences for the ski resort. These consequences will range from large positive consequences when snowfalls are high, to large negative consequences when snowfalls fail to occur. This can be shown on the horizontal axis in Figure 1.1, using a scale showing the $ variation from budgeted profit, from a positive profit variance of $8 million to negative $8 million. The positive $8 million may arise where future snowfalls are very high, averaging say 30 cm per day, throughout the season. The likelihood of this occurring, which is shown on the vertical axis, is however very low (near to zero per cent). Equally the occurrence of a negative $8 million variance from budget which may arise when no future snow falls occur throughout the season, is equally as unlikely. The most likely, with a probability of occurrence of 20 per cent (0.2), is to achieve budget ($ zero variance).

Figure 1.1 illustrates:

1. The range of potential *consequences* that could result if the risk were to occur along the horizontal axis. For this example, the potential consequences range from large positive, through zero, to large negative consequences. Each type of risk will have a different potential range of consequences. Risks may have:

   a. Negative consequences only. For example, a health pandemic risk to a non-pharmaceutical company would only have potential negative consequences.
   b. Positive consequences only. For example, the risk of a new office block being constructed close to an existing sandwich shop is most likely to have only potential positive consequences for that shop in terms of profitability as tenants move in and increase sales.
   c. Positive and negative consequences. For example, a health pandemic risk to a pharmaceutical company has potential negative consequences through affecting the company's own workforce but also a potential positive consequence in terms of increased sales.

   The majority of operational risks are in the first category, that is, negative consequences only. The range of potential consequences will also differ between risk types. Some risks will have a narrow range of potential consequences while others will have a much wider range.

2. *Exposure* to a risk occurs where the potential consequence is other than zero, that is, there are potential consequences across the horizontal axis. If the risk has zero potential consequence then there is no *exposure* to that risk.

3. The *likelihood* of each consequence occurring is shown on the vertical axis. For this example, we can see that the most likely outcome is a small positive or negative consequence, while large positive and negative consequences have a much lower likelihood of occurrence. For each risk, there will be a level of consequence that is most likely and as you move away from that point, the likelihood progressively reduces.

4. The analysis of likelihood and consequence must take place for a given *future time period*. This may range from minutes to years, depending on the length of the exposure. The time period or 'risk horizon' needs to be determined before likelihood and consequence can be accurately assessed.

DEFINING OPERATIONAL RISK

The scope of operational risk is vast, covering literally thousands of different risks. Capturing it in a single definition is a challenge. As a result, definitions abound. The world banking regulator (Basel Committee) defines operational risk in the Basel II regulatory framework as:

> *The risk of loss from failed or inadequate processes, people, systems or external events.*

> *(Basel Committee on Banking Supervision, Internal Convergence of Capital Measurement and Capital Standards, June 2006, 144)*

This definition is somewhat narrow as:

1. It mentions the risk of loss only. There is no mention of the potential for opportunity, positive consequence or gain.

2. *'Loss'* is not defined.

When working with clients we encourage them to develop their own definition which works best for them. As an example, an alternative definition might be:

> *The risk of loss or gain arising from people, systems or external events which have the potential to cause the organisation to deviate from its objectives.*

This definition recognises that:

1. Operational risk refers to the deviation from achieving the set objectives. The loss or gain therefore may be a financial loss (affecting a profit objective) or a non-financial loss (affecting a non financial objective such as customer satisfaction).

2. Operational risk comes from three main sources:

   a. People. This covers deliberate and non-deliberate actions.
   b. Systems. This covers any risk arising from a non-human, physical (for example, a table) or non-physical (for example, software) object.
   c. External events. This covers all risks that are external to the organisation such as acts of nature, changes in legislation and failed suppliers.

DIFFERENTIATING OPERATIONAL RISK FROM OTHER RISKS

Total risk for an organisation covers all risks that could potentially affect the achievement of the organisation's objectives. For many organisations, total risk is often subdivided into four or five major risks. As an example, these may be:

- Operational Risk

- Market/Financial Risk

- Credit Risk

- Liquidity Risk

- Strategic Risk.

Market/Financial Risk may be defined as: *'The risk of profit or loss due to a potential change in market prices, such as Interest Rates, Foreign Exchange Rates, Commodity Prices and Equity Prices.'*

Credit Risk may be defined as: *'The risk of loss arising from a third party not meeting their obligations to make payments to the organisation when they are due.'*

Liquidity Risk may be defined as: *'The risk of not being able to transact in a market at all or only at a significant cost / loss due to a lack of demand and supply in that market.'*

This risk arises primarily from:

● Funds Risk – Not being able to meet cash obligations as they fall due.

● Transactions Risk – Not being able to transact in illiquid markets without significant cost or loss, including the inability to borrow at reasonable interest rates.

Strategic Risk may be defined as: *'The risk of deciding on and following incorrect strategies, of not executing the strategies successfully and the impact that the strategies will have on the business risk profile once implemented. Strategic risk can therefore be broken down into three parts as follows:*

1. *Strategic Decision Risk – The risk of not selecting and following the optimal strategy to achieve our objectives. This risk takes into account the impact of external changes which may be known, partially known or unknown at the time the decisions are made.*

2. *Execution Risk – The risk of not executing the strategies successfully.*

3. *Delivered Risk – The impact that the strategies may have on ongoing business risks, once the strategies are delivered.'*

A key characteristic that distinguishes different risks is whether the risk has the potential for both upside and downside, or whether there is primarily downside potential only. Market risk for example, as can be seen in Figure 1.2, has relatively equal potential for upside and downside. The purchase of a share in a company creates exposure to equity price risk. This would result in a profit if the share price were to rise and a loss if it were to fall.

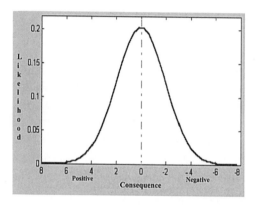

Figure 1.2   Probability distribution for market risk

Other risks, such as the majority of operational risks, have downside potential only as is illustrated in Figure 1.3. As an example, to the majority of organisations, the failure of IT systems can only bring downside.

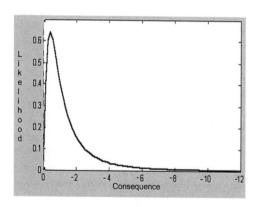

Figure 1.3   Probability distribution for operational risk (failure of IT systems)

There are some operational risks that may have upside potential to specific organisations. Examples are as follows:

1. A company may accidentally buy 100,000 shares in a company rather than 10,000 due to human error. Over the period until the excess 90,000 shares are sold, the shares may increase in value yielding a profit from the error. It has to be noted that this is due to luck rather than an intention by the person to make a deliberate error in order to make money.

2. Where one operational risk, such as a pandemic, may be a downside risk to one organisation, it will also be an upside risk to pharmaceutical companies who produce the vaccines.

OPERATIONAL RISK MANAGEMENT

Risk management is the process of managing risk. Within an organisation, the management of all risk is often referred to 'Enterprise Risk Management (ERM)'. For most organisations, operational risk management forms the largest component of ERM.

Enterprise risk management is constantly practised by all organisations and employees on a day-to-day intuitive basis. These practices represent the informal, everyday, end of the risk management spectrum. As the risks involved become larger for the organisation, risk management tends to move towards a more formal process. The informal to formal boundary needs to be recognised.

Enterprise Risk Management can be defined as:

'... a process, effected by an entity's board of directors, management and other personnel, applied in strategy setting and across the enterprise, designed to identify potential events that may affect the entity, and manage risks to be within its risk appetite, to provide reasonable assurance regarding the achievement of entity objectives.'

Source: COSO Enterprise Risk Management
– Integrated Framework. COSO, 2004

This definition captures the key elements of operational risk management. These are analysed as follows:

KEY ELEMENTS OF RISK MANAGEMENT

Process: It must be an embedded process within the day-to-day activities of the organisation rather than as an ad hoc review or a 'project'.

Effected by an entity's board of directors, management and other personnel: Risk management is the responsibility of 'everyone' within an organisation, not just of the specialist risk managers.

Risk appetite: An essential part of risk management is for the organisation to set its appetite or tolerance for risk.

Reasonable assurance: Risk management can only provide reasonable assurance and not a 100 per cent guarantee. This is because there are no guarantees that a risk will never occur.

Entity's objectives: Risk management is strongly focussed on ensuring the organisation meets its objectives.

THE OBJECTIVES OF OPERATIONAL RISK MANAGEMENT

The specific objectives in managing operational risk will differ between organisations but will most commonly include one or more of the following::

- reducing avoidable losses

- reducing insurance costs

- protecting and enhancing reputation

- protecting and improving credit rating

- improving risk and control culture

- improving awareness, objectivity, transparency and accountability of risk

- improving the efficiency and effectiveness of controls and processes

- providing greater levels of assurance to management

- assisting management in meeting external requirements

- identifying opportunities relating to risk.

OPERATIONAL RISK CAUSES, EVENTS, EFFECTS AND CONTROLS

The meaning of 'an operational risk' may differ considerably between people as 'risk' is not a single concept but instead has a number of interlinking components or stages.

For example, consider the following: while driving to work there is the potential for a stone to be thrown up by a passing vehicle, hitting the radiator and piercing a hole in it. As a result, the water leaks out, the engine overheats and the car stops. The driver is then late for work and receives a sizeable repair bill for fixing the engine.

This complete description is a 'risk story' or 'risk statement'. It is made up of a number of components being:

Operational risk cause: This is the initial starting point of the risk story. In this example, it is the stone being thrown up by a passing vehicle.

Operational risk event(s): These are the subsequent occurrences that then happen as a result of the cause having occurred. In this example, these would be:

- a hole in the radiator

- water leaking out

- engine overheating

- car stopping

- the driver being unable to get to work.

Risk effects: These are the final impacts of the risk story, representing a deviation from the driver's expected objectives. In the example these were:

- The driver being late for work. The driver's objective was to arrive at work on time.

- The cost of repairs. One of the driver's objectives would be to control/minimise the cost of travel.

A risk story therefore has a start (cause), a middle (event) and an end (effects). In each risk story, there may be one or more causes, events and effects.

IDENTIFYING CAUSES, EVENTS AND EFFECTS

There are a number of techniques available to assist in identifying risk causes, events and effects in any given risk story. As examples, these include fishbone diagrams and bow tie diagrams (see Figures 1.4 and 1.6).

As an illustration, the fishbone diagram for the vehicle example above is shown in Figure 1.5. This demonstrates the linkage between causes, events and effects.

Figure 1.6 again demonstrates the linkage between causes, events and effects but focuses on analysing the causes and effects of one prime event.

One of my favoured techniques is the 'But Why? and What Next?' approach. This operates as follows:

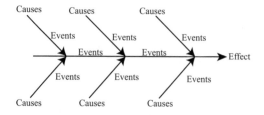

Figure 1.4   Fishbone diagram

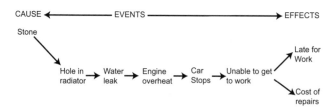

Figure 1.5   Example of a fishbone diagram

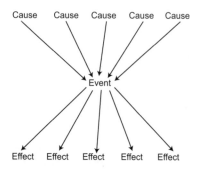

Figure 1.6   Bowtie diagram

1. First, a risk event is identified. Commonly, the most easily identified component of a risk story is a risk event. In the previous motor vehicle example this would most likely be the engine stopping as it would be the first thing that the driver notices.

2. Secondly, the question 'But Why?' is asked until either:

   a. There is no further plausible answer and/or
   b. The answer relates to an event which is outside of the organisation's or persons' control.

This is the *cause*. This is known as 'causal analysis' or 'root cause analysis'.

Applying this analysis to the motor vehicle example:

Step 1. The event is the engine stopping.

Step 2. But why did the engine stop? – Because the engine overheated.

Step 3. But why did the engine overheat? – Because water leaked out of the radiator.

Step 4. But why did water leak out of the radiator? – Because there was a hole in it.

Step 5. But why is there a hole in the radiator? – Because a stone hit it after being thrown up by another vehicle.

Step 6. This is the *cause* as the reason for the stone being kicked up is outside of the driver's control (you cannot stop other vehicles from passing you!).

3. Thirdly, ask the question 'What happens next?' until there is no further meaningful answer or the connection to the answer is weak.

Step 7. What happens next after the engine stops? – The driver is not able to get to work.

Step 8. What happens next after not being able to get to work? – The driver is late for work.

Step 9. What happens next to correct the problem? – The driver receives a sizeable repair bill

Steps 8 and 9 are the *effects*. In this example there are two effects and these can be viewed in terms of deviations from the expected outcome of the process of driving to work.

CONTROLS OVER OPERATIONAL RISK

A 'Control' is defined in the ISO 31000: *Risk Management Standard* as a 'Measure that is modifying risk'.

Controls are usually taken to mean a measure that reduces risk, either by reducing the likelihood of the risk occurring and/or reducing the consequence when it does occur.

There are three main types of controls (Figure 1.7) depending on their type of risk impact:

Preventive controls: These controls prevent risk causes or events from occurring. For example, the segregation of incompatible duties or password access controls on IT systems.

21

Detective controls: These controls detect event(s) that have occurred, and together with follow-up actions, aim to stop or limit any potential impact. For example, the reconciliation of data seeks to identify discrepancies. A smoke detector seeks to identify smoke in the early stages of a fire.

Reactive–remedial controls: These controls are aimed at mitigating the size of the impact. For example, business continuity planning seeks to minimise the impact of business disruptions and insurance seeks to minimise the impact of insurable events when they occur.

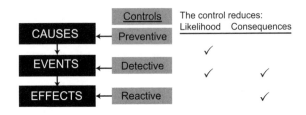

Figure 1.7   Control types

THE LIFECYCLE OF RISK

Risk has a time-based lifecycle, from being a remote potential risk (future risk), to being a risk that is presently occurring (current risk), through to the risk actually occurring and causing a risk incident (risk incident).

Consider the various operational risks to be like raindrops falling into a funnel as illustrated in Figure 1.8.

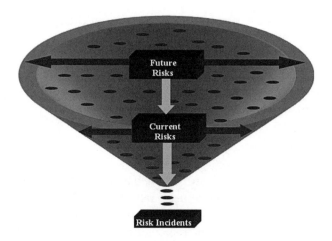

Figure 1.8   The lifecycle of risk

FUTURE RISKS

Future risks are potential risks that could, but may not, occur. At this stage of the risk lifecycle, they have not yet occurred. There are many risks at this level which is represented by a wide funnel entrance.

In the motor vehicle example, this would be the potential for the radiator to be punctured.

CURRENT RISKS

Current risks are risks where the *risk story* has commenced. That is, a risk cause has occurred and, in addition, one or more risk events may have eventuated. At this stage, no impact on objectives has occurred. In Figure 1.8 these risks are represented by the middle section of the funnel. There are less risks now, represented by a narrower part of the funnel, as not all future potential risks will actually occur.

In the example, a *current risk* would be where the engine is beginning to overheat but the engine has not yet seized and stopped.

RISK INCIDENTS

A risk incident is a risk story that has taken place and either one or more impacts have been felt. A risk incident may also be a 'near miss'. This is where no impact has been felt and the risk story has finished. The risk incident did however have the potential to result in one or more impacts. Risk incidents are represented by risks falling out of the bottom of the funnel.

In the example, this is where the engine has now seized and stopped. The driver cannot get to work, and cost is incurred to fix the engine.

Risk will always follow the cycle of cause, event and effect even though we may not be aware of the risk either passing through, or being at, each stage.

OPERATIONAL RISK AWARENESS

Being aware of the range of risks to which an individual or organisation is exposed is the first stage of being able to manage risk. You cannot manage something of which you are not aware.

There are three levels of risk awareness:

Level 1: Known Risk – 'We know what we know': These are risks of which the organisation has first-hand experience. As a result, risk awareness is high. These risks tend to have a higher likelihood of occurrence and lower consequence when they do occur. An example would be a staff member being absent due to illness.

Level 2: Knowable Risk – 'We know what we don't know': These are risks about which the organisation has no first-hand experience but is aware that others have experienced this risk. Risk awareness and acceptance is lower in most organisations as humans tend to have the view that 'it will not happen to me'. These risks tend to have a lower likelihood of occurrence but larger consequences when they do occur. An example would be a building fire.

Level 3: Unknowable Risk – 'We don't know what we don't know': These are risks about which the organisation has no first-hand experience, neither are they aware of others having ever experienced this risk. Risk awareness and acceptance is very low to the point that often people take the view that such a risk will never happen. These risks tend to have a very low likelihood of occurrence but very large consequences when they do occur. An example may be an earthquake in an area of low seismic activity.

CONCLUSION

In this chapter we have analysed the components and nature of operational risk so that we can better understand this complex concept. The breakdown of operational risk into causes, events and effects and into its lifecycle stages provides a better understanding of how risk behaves and as a result helps in the design of relevant processes to manage that risk.

The next chapter covers the concept of risk management frameworks which provide the structure in which robust risk management processes can be developed.

② Frameworks for Managing Operational Risk

Above all other skills, managing operational risk requires common sense. However, due to the extensive scope of operational risk and its many components, a substantial depth of common sense is required, which needs to be ordered into simple, logical steps. These steps constitute the various risk management frameworks and standards that have been developed.

Informal operational risk management frameworks have been in place since the beginning of time. These frameworks are usually undocumented and exist in the way people think and react to given situations. Such informal frameworks lack consistency, accountability and quality assurance.

A formal risk management framework applied to an organisation provides the following key benefits:

- Consistency in the approach to, and quality of, managing all operational risks.

- Consistency in risk language.

- The ability to consolidate and compare risk information from different parts of the organisation.

- A basis for increasing risk knowledge and skills.

- A basis for developing and maintaining a strong risk and control culture.

There are many risk management models, methodologies, frameworks, standards and sources of guidance that have developed over the last ten to 15 years. This is a common feature of a rapidly developing discipline, such as operational risk management.

The following discussion provides an insight into current operational risk management frameworks and standards.

THE 'THREE LINES OF DEFENCE' FRAMEWORK

The 'Three Lines of Defence' framework (Figure 2.1) describes how risk should be managed by an organisation. The framework firstly considers *Inherent Risks*. Inherent risks are those risks that are inherent in the activity or process being undertaken and that are an integral and inseparable part of that activity. The level of inherent risk is the risk prior to considering the effect of any risk treatment methods, that is, a raw risk that has had no mitigation factors or treatments applied.

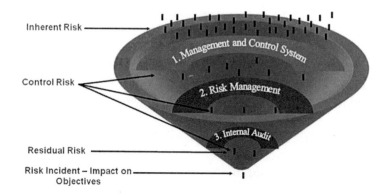

Figure 2.1   The three lines of defence

By way of illustration, consider the activity of walking in the open air. Rain would be an inherent risk which would affect your level of comfort. The inherent level of rain risk may be determined by assessing the likelihood of rain occurring and if it were to occur, what level of discomfort would be felt. This is most likely to be dependent on how hard the rain falls.

The lines of defence against this 'rain risk' are as follows:

DEFENCE LINE 1: THE MANAGEMENT AND CONTROL SYSTEM

The first line of defence can be illustrated as an umbrella. This does not reduce the likelihood or intensity of rain but it does protect us against the effect of rain if it were to occur. Within the business environment, this is the internal control system covering all of the procedures that are designed to manage and control the inherent risks.

DEFENCE LINE 2: RISK MANAGEMENT

The second line of defence is a check that our umbrella is sound prior to going outside. This would include checks of the umbrella covering for holes and the soundness of the support frame.

In business, the second line of defence is represented by the organisation's enterprise risk management systems and procedures, including the compliance function.

DEFENCE LINE 3: INTERNAL AUDIT

The third line of defence would be represented by an independent party reviewing the umbrella. They would act as an additional level of assurance that the umbrella was sound.

In business, this line of defence is represented by the internal audit function. This function is an independent, objective assurance and consulting activity designed to evaluate and improve the effectiveness of risk management, control and governance processes.

The level of risk, after considering the first line of defence, is known as residual risk. In the rain example, the residual rain risk is the degree to which you are still getting wet notwithstanding the umbrella you are using.

The relationship between inherent and residual risk can be demonstrated as:

Inherent Risk   IR

Less: The effectiveness of controls   (C)

Equals Residual Risk   **RR**

Where the effectiveness of controls is inadequate and leads to unacceptably high levels of residual risk, this control ineffectiveness is often referred to as 'control risk'. Control risk is the risk that the management and control system, risk management and internal audit, fail to identify and/or manage the risk adequately. This can be illustrated as the umbrella leaking.

RISK MANAGEMENT STANDARDS

There have been a number of risk management standards, principles and guidelines that have been developed over the past ten to 15 years. These standards and guidelines are focused either on risk management generally, or on specific types of risk, such as information technology risk. In December 2009, ISO 31000:2009 Risk Management – Principles and Guidelines was issued. This represented the first global generic risk management standard. This standard was developed over a four- to five-year period commencing in 2005 when the International Organization for Standardization (ISO) established a working group to develop the first international risk management standard. The standard used the Australian and New Zealand AS/NZS 4360: 2004 *Risk Management Standard* as the first draft.

The ISO 31000 principles and guidelines for risk management, establishes:

Risk Management Principles. The risk management principles cover the key attributes that should be present in an effective risk management framework. As examples, these principles recommend that risk management needs to be:

- integrated into the organisation's processes

- included as an important part of decision making

- formal, being structured and systematic

- tailored to the specific nature of the organisation

- dynamic and continually improved.

Risk Management Framework. The standard highlights that the development of a risk management framework should include a number of steps. One of the most important is the initial stage of obtaining the mandate and commitment of the board of directors and senior management for establishing and supporting a risk management function. Once this is achieved, the framework then needs to be designed, implemented, continually monitored and reviewed and improved.

Risk Management Processes. The process steps contained in the ISO 31000 Standard to conduct risk management have largely been extracted from the AS/NZS 4360: 2004 *Risk Management Standard* (superseded by AS/NZS ISO 31000:2009). These steps include:

- **Communicate and consult** – This step involves engaging the organisation's stakeholders such as shareholders and regulators and understanding their objectives and requirements for risk management of the entity.

- **Establish the context** – This step involves gaining an understanding of the overall context within which risk management will be conducted. This will include such aspects as the organisation's objectives, culture, environment, strengths and weaknesses.

- **Identify risks** – This stage involves one or more processes to allow continual identification of the risks to which the organisation is exposed.

- **Analyse risks** – Once the risks have been identified, this step involves an analysis as to the likelihood of occurrence and the consequence if the risk were to occur. This leads to an assessment as to the overall 'size' of the risk and of its relative importance to other risks.

- **Evaluate risks** – Once the risk is analysed and its 'size' determined, the risk needs to be assessed against predetermined levels to determine whether it is within the risk appetite–tolerance of the organisation and, if not, what level of escalation is required.

- **Risk treatment** – Once the various operational risks have been identified and measured, they may need to be treated. The treatment of operational risks includes the following techniques:

  - *Risk acceptance*: this occurs where no further treatment is implemented and the current level of risk is formally accepted.
  - *Modifying Controls*: modifying either likelihood and-or consequence reducing controls. This may either reduce or increase the risk compared to current levels.

- *Risk avoidance*: this involves ceasing the activity that is causing the risk.
- *Risk transfer*: this involves the consequence of the risk being transferred to a third party, such as insurance.
- *Risk commencement or risk increase*: this can occur when controls are relaxed or removed as they may be inefficient or curtailing business, or where a process is reengineered and new risks arrive.
- *Risk transformation*: this occurs where one or more risks are transformed into one or more other risks. This is a combination of risk avoidance and risk commencement. An example would be where a manual process is outsourced. This eliminates human error risk but intoduces a new 'failure of outsource supplier risk.

- **Monitor and review** – Operational risk is dynamic and ever changing. This step requires a process of ongoing monitoring and review to ensure risks are continually identified, analysed, evaluated and treated.

- **Record the risk management process** – The risk management process needs to be formally recorded much like the accountant must record transactions in a general ledger. The risk manager should record the risks in a formal record. This may consist of a number or records such as risk and hazard registers, risk incident records, risk indicator recording and compliance attestation records.

CONCLUSION

Risk management frameworks provide an essential overarching methodology which ensures that all of the detailed operational risk processes and practices operated within an organisation are cohesive and work together. A framework also assists in operational risk understanding, particularly in relation to why specific risk management practices are followed and how they fit into the bigger picture. Lastly, frameworks backed up by standards, provide a benchmark against which an organisation can assess how their risk management measures up and provides guidance as to what best practice risk management should look like.

The next chapter looks at the essential elements that need to be in place within an organisation in order to implement robust operational risk management. This includes the right resources, the right organisation structure and the right risk and control culture.

③ Operational Risk Management in the Corporate Structure

For most organisations, operational risk is usually the largest risk exposure faced. Traditionally the functions relating to the management of operational risk are managed independently and are not integrated within the one discipline of 'operational risk management'. These functions include:

- insurance

- legal

- occupational health and safety

- security

- fraud management

- disaster recovery and business continuity

- compliance.

Operational risk management as a discipline has now developed to the stage where there should be a recognised formal operational risk management function which consolidates all of the disparate risk management activities into one cohesive and coordinated group. This approach usually involves the appointment of a 'Head of Operational Risk Management' which reports to a Chief Risk Officer. Depending on the size of the organisation, there would typically be:

- A Group Operational Risk team which supports the Head of Operational Risk at the corporate level;

- Business risk managers operating in each business unit being dedicated to operational risk management at the more granular level; and

- The specialist risk areas such as legal and insurance continuing to operate substantially as before, but with formal/informal reporting lines to the head of operational risk management.

Figure 3.1   Example organisation chart for operational risk management

THE ROLES AND RESPONSIBILITIES FOR RISK MANAGEMENT

Case Study

A South African client made it very clear as to who is responsible for operational risk management with posters as shown in Figure 3.2 posted throughout the organisation. The message is that operational risk management is the responsibility of everyone, not just of a select few.

Figure 3.2   Responsibility for operational risk management

The specific responsibilities, activities and functions with respect to operational risk management of each area within an organisation, as shown in Figure 3.1, will obviously differ based on size, business organisation structure, nature of the business and so on. The following provides an overview of the typical responsibilities and functions of each area.

1. **Board.** Responsible for:

- Understanding the key operational risks to which the organisation is exposed;
- Overseeing the implementation and maintenance of a robust operational risk management framework;
- Providing oversight to the risk management process. Receiving, reviewing and actioning reports. Overseeing major risk issues;
- Setting the organisation's operational risk appetite–tolerance;
- Approving the operational risk management policies; and
- Setting and encouraging an appropriate operational risk culture.

2. **Executive Management.** Responsible for:

- Implementing a robust operational risk management framework; and
- Receiving and actioning operational risk management reports.

3. **Operational Risk Committee (ORC).** The typical committee will be responsible for:

- Developing a committee charter;
- Receiving and reviewing regular risk reports;
- Reviewing, assessing and following up key risk information such as:
  - risks outside of appetite
  - key risk indicators in the high zone
  - risk incidents above certain thresholds for size or type
  - improvement actions overdue
  - negative or missing compliance attestations; and

- Preparing and approving the board risk report.

4. **Internal Audit**. Responsible for:

- Providing independent objective assurance over the risk management, control and governance of the organisation; and
- Evaluating and improving the effectiveness of risk management, controls and governance.

Internal audit should NOT be directly responsible for operational risk management. Internal audit is an independent third line of defence separate from the first line (business) and second line (risk management). As it is responsible for auditing the second line (risk management), it cannot also be part of risk management. This feature is specifically brought out in the banking industry where the world banking regulator, the Basel Committee, specifically states in Principle 2 of the 'Sound Practices for the Management and Supervision of Operational Risk', that internal

- Supporting the business units in their risk-related responsibilities;
- Being the liaison point between the business units and group operational risk (GOR);
- Training business unit staff in risk-related matters;
- Being the 'centre of excellence' for operational risk management in the business units; and
- Ensuring a degree of independence between the business units and the operational risk management function.

INDEPENDENCE OF OPERATIONAL RISK MANAGEMENT

A key aspect of the 'Three Lines of Defence' model that was described in Chapter 2 is the independence that exists between each line of defence. That is:

1. Internal audit should be independent from operational risk management and the business. This point was discussed under the role of internal audit earlier.

2. Operational risk management should be independent of the business. This means that operational risk management should have independence of decision making separate from the businesses which are being risk managed. This can be achieved through business risk managers reporting directly to GOR. The experience of organisations who followed this approach often involved the business seeing the risk managers as 'just another auditor' leading to a lack of engagement and support for operational risk management from the business. In order to overcome

this we now most commonly see an independent group function with business risk managers reporting to the business unit to which they are attached. The business risk manager also has an informal reporting line to GOR. We are often asked by clients 'Is our structure "independent"?' Our standard answer is: 'If a risk issue is raised by the business risk manager who believes it should be reported to GOR and the business unit manager requests suppression, what will the risk manager do?' If the answer is 'report', then independence exists. If the answer is 'not report', independence does not exist.

OPERATIONAL RISK APPETITE AND TOLERANCE

The setting of an organisation's risk 'appetite' is a critical component of operational risk management. It enables risks to be 'evaluated' against the appetite and a mechanism for escalating and treating risks that fall outside of the appetite. The 'appetite' should be set by the organisation's board of directors, or equivalent, and reflect the board's level of appetite for operational risk.

Case Study

Setting operational risk appetite. I remember, some years ago, working with a board for the first time in trying to set an operational risk appetite. My question was *'What is your operational risk appetite?'* I was met with blank faces and a barrage of questions including:

'What do you mean?'

'How do we do that?'

'We have no appetite for operational risk, we would prefer no operational risk at all.'

'How do we articulate that?'

'We want to get rid of all of it'

This experience promoted me to consider further as to what risk appetite means for a board, how it could be better articulated, and what approach could be used to determine that appetite. The following is the result, with which I have experienced much higher levels of success:

1. Boards mostly view operational risk as a 'bad' thing. That is, it most often leads to negative consequences. Therefore asking the question 'Do you have an appetite for something bad?', the response will inevitably be 'NO!'. I often use the analogy of being faced with a plate of freshly made muffins and a jar of wriggling earth worms. Most of us would have a literal 'appetite' for the muffins as they taste good. That is, there is a positive consequence from consuming. But we may limit our intake to one muffin as we are also aware of the detrimental effects to our waist line. That is, they have a negative consequence too! 'Appetite' for something with an upside consequence makes sense. On the other hand, I would suggest that very few people would have an appetite for consuming the earth worms. However, if you were to receive $1 million if you ate the earth worms, would you do it? I would suggest that a fair proportion of us would eat the worms – why? Because we are willing to 'tolerate' the negative consequence of the bad taste

and the risk of making us ill, so that we can achieve the reward. Operational risk predominantly works like the earth worms. We have to tolerate some operational risk in order to achieve our business objectives. Therefore it makes more sense to use the word 'tolerance' when setting operational risk appetite.

2. For some risks, organisations usually have zero tolerance. These most often involve:

- Risks arising from deliberate acts of staff such as:
  - internal fraud
  - harassment
  - inappropriate internet usage.

We often use the cliché 'give a person an inch, they will take a mile'. Because these acts are deliberately initiated by humans, they need to be eliminated completely.

- Risks where the consequence is so large that one single occurrence cannot be tolerated. An example may be the breach of a key regulatory requirement that could lead to loss of an operating licence.

3. The level of tolerance should be articulated in measurable terms rather than subjective statements such as 'high', 'medium', or 'low'. In order for risk managers to be able to evaluate the actual level of risk against these tolerances, they must be articulated in a measureable way. Examples of how these tolerances may be articulated are as follows:

- The setting of thresholds for key risk indicators. This is covered in Chapter 6.

- The setting of the risk level zones when reporting the results of the risk and control self assessment process. This is covered in Chapter 5.

4. Logically, if a risk will provide only negative consequences, we would want to eliminate it. However, unless we have zero tolerance, the diminishing ratio of the benefit to cost of continually increasing controls will make it uneconomical to eliminate all risk, even if it were possible. Theoretically at least, there will be a point where the marginal cost of additional control will equal the marginal benefit of increased control. At this point we should stop, hopefully with the risk within our tolerance. If the risk is not within tolerance, additional treatment methods such as formal acceptance or avoidance need to be considered.

We now have much greater success in getting boards to articulate meaningful tolerance levels which can then be used in the risk framework to evaluate risks.

RISK POLICIES AND PROCEDURES

The operational risk framework needs to be supported by operational risk policies and procedures. A typical structure showing how operational risk management policies fit in with overall risk policies is shown in Figure 3.3.

The group risk policy provides an overarching policy for all risks within the organisation. This will encapsulate not only operational risks but also financial risks such as credit, market and liquidity.

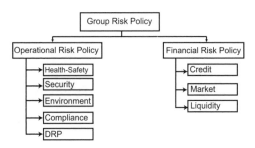

Figure 3.3   Structure of operational risk management policies

The operational risk policy should sit under the group risk policy and cover all policy matters concerning operational risk management. Sub risk policies covering specialist risk areas such as health and safety, environmental risk and so on are commonly included as a subset to the overall operational risk management policy.

The content of the operational risk management policy will vary substantially between different organisations. A comprehensive policy would ordinarily include:

- definition of operational risk

- risk categorisation framework including risk causes, risk events and risk effects

- objectives of operational risk management in the organisation

- organisation structure for operational risk management including responsibilities, reporting lines, authorities and role of specialist risk units

- risk appetite-tolerance

- operational risk management framework

- risk and control self assessment policies

- key risk indicator policies

- incident management and recording policies

- external and internal compliance policies

- risk treatment and continual improvement policies

- reporting and escalations

- risk systems

- regulatory considerations

- crisis management

- risk culture

- staff training.

Like any policy, the operational risk management policies should be concise, focusing on policy matters only, rather than procedural matters.

As for any other activity, the operational risk management process should be documented. This usually incorporates procedures manuals which set a granular level view of the various procedures which make up the operational risk management process.

RISK AND CONTROL CULTURE

Much is written about risk and control culture and its importance in creating a strong operational risk management framework. Unfortunately, for many organisations, risk culture often gets scant attention. However, risk and control culture within an organisation is usually the single most important factor in determining the success or otherwise of the operational risk management process. Without it, everything else can be rendered ineffective. It acts as a solid foundation on which a robust risk management framework and function can be built.

The cliché, 'you can take a horse to water but you cannot make it drink' is very relevant to operational risk management. You can take a good operational risk framework, systems and processes to management but you cannot make them use it. The desire to use it is the outcome of a good risk culture.

FEATURES OF RISK AND CONTROL CULTURE

1. Culture is based in a person's belief system, not on paper.

2. Individuals have different cultural norms. The organisation must develop its own culture separate from its individuals. For example, the views of staff members as to what behaviour is seen as acceptable and unacceptable will most likely be wide ranging. Clear cultural boundaries need to be defined as to what the organisation sees as acceptable and unacceptable.

3. Many individuals need rules and boundaries. Apart from an organisation's true leaders, most individuals require some rules and boundaries to work within. Risk and control culture provide these.

4. Culture is manifested in attitudes, beliefs and behaviour. This will cover many things such as:

- Attitude to freeness of communication.
- Level of honesty and integrity.
- Attitude to compliance attestations.
- Time to complacency; this is a measure of how long it would take for an individual to stop carrying out a control if they were left on their own to ensure that it was performed.

Case Study

Time to complacency. Many years ago a very experienced hang glider pilot with many thousands of flights to his name died in a gliding accident not from, as you might expect, a highly skilled manoeuvre that went wrong. On learning to hang glide, one of the first controls you ever learn is the 'hang check'. This is to suspend yourself from the glider while it is on the ground to ensure you are correctly attached. The pilot had followed this procedure many thousands of times but on this one occasion he forgot, only realising the mistake once airborne, by which time it was too late. Even though the time to complacency was long in this instance, overlooking the control was costly.

5. Attitude to taking responsibility. Taking responsibility for risk and the related controls is essential. An attitude of

'that is not my problem' or 'that is someone else's problem' shows poor risk and control culture.

A MEASURE OF RISK AND CONTROL CULTURE

It can be difficult to gauge the level of risk and control culture in an organisation other than from an opinion formed during time spent with staff and management. However, a 'risk culture questionnaire' can be useful to gain some understanding quickly. This may include such questions as:

- Why are you doing that control?

- What is operational risk?

- When did you last review your controls?

- When did you last consider the risks that you face?

- What are the key risk drivers of your business?

- If a problem occurs, will you tend to keep it to yourself or immediately report it?

DEVELOPING AND MAINTAINING A STRONG RISK AND CONTROL CULTURE

In order to develop and maintain a strong risk and control culture, the following approaches should be considered:

1. Top down, bottom up. Culture should be set by a 'tone at the top' with the correct messages and examples being set by the Board and senior management. In addition, culture

should be instilled at every level including the most junior members of staff.

2. Educate staff. Staff should be educated in a range of risk and control matters including:

- Understanding risk.
- Risk awareness.
- The reason for performing controls, rather than staff just doing them because they were told to. Controls are not hoops to jump through but have a valid business purpose to control a risk that has the potential to cause underperformance.

3. Controls should be regularly reviewed for ongoing relevance and efficiency.

Case Study

Irrelevant controls. As part of a client assignment, reconciliation controls were being reviewed in the finance department. One particular reconciliation involved comparing the totals from two different reports. On questioning the control, the reconciliation clerk commented that it was a good control as she had not had any discrepancies in over a year. On further investigation, it was found that the two reports were generated from the same system and the same database and therefore could never be different. The control had been put in place when two different systems produced the reports. However, around 12 months earlier, a new system had been introduced, hence the lack of discrepancies! As you can imagine, the clerk was despondent in that she had been carrying out a pointless control for 12 months.

4. Encourage staff to suggest control and procedural improvements. This encourages creative thinking and ownership. Often the most knowledgeable person regarding the risks of an activity is the person responsible for it.

5. Integrate risk culture into day-to-day practices. This should include risk information being used visibly in decision making. If staff see their risk output being used it will create a positive attitude to operational risk management.

6. Operational risk policies should be relevant, readable and concise.

7. Good risk and control culture should be encouraged through an incentive scheme.

8. Consistent behaviour should be shown especially with respect to management reacting to culture and risk issues.

Case Study

Inconsistent behaviour. A company at which one of my course attendees worked, had a zero tolerance policy to indecent materials including inappropriate internet usage and any other written or electronic media brought into the office. Two junior staff members in the participant's department were caught using the internet inappropriately and under the company policy were dismissed. Sometime later the participant's boss took annual leave and she was responsible for collecting his mail. On returning one day she accidentally dropped the mail only to see indecent magazines spill onto the pavement. Suffice to say she reported it according to company policy but it was kept quiet and no action ever taken against the senior manager. She quickly lost respect for the organisation.

CONCLUSION

This chapter has highlighted the essential internal elements that an organisation needs in order to provide a strong foundation on which to build robust operational risk management practices. This foundation must consist of the right human resources organised in the most effective way, a range of coordinated operational risk management specialists, strong policies and procedures supporting the operational risk management practices and, above all, a strong risk and control culture that permeates throughout the organisation and ensures a high number of staff are engaged with, and legitimise, the operational risk management function.

The next chapter develops a series of operational risk management processes that act as the practical day-to-day application of a strong operational risk management framework.

PART 2

A Methodology to Manage Operational Risk

Components of an Operational Risk Management Framework

Operational risk has been in existence since the beginning of time arising from humankind's simple actions and interactions with the environment. As a result, many informal and formal risk management methods and techniques have been developed through the ages. It has however been only in the last twenty years or so that widely accepted formal operational risk management methodologies have developed. These methodologies have been both driven by, and culminated in, risk management standards, principles and guidelines that have promoted widespread consistent approaches to operational risk management.

Figure 4.1   Operational risk management of a motor vehicle

As organisations are often very different in their objectives, the activities they undertake and the way they are managed, a risk management methodology at the micro level needs to be tailored to each organisation. Certain differences in methodologies will therefore be essential.

The following provides an example of an operational risk management methodology, highlighting the key components which are widely accepted as being core to a comprehensive framework. The methodology will be considered in relation to an activity most of us will be familiar with, that of running a motor vehicle.

AN EXAMPLE OF MANAGING OPERATIONAL RISK – A MOTOR VEHICLE (FIGURE 4.1)

FUTURE RISKS AND THE VEHICLE SERVICE

The scope of future potential risks in relation to operating a motor vehicle is extensive. These range from such mechanical things as brake failure, broken windscreen and engine seizure, to driver related risks such as running out of fuel and accidents. In relation to the management of future potential mechanical based risks, the main risk management process is the periodic car service. A qualified mechanic carries out checks on the car which identifies risks and where the level is unacceptable, carries out repairs and/or provides a repair schedule.

CURRENT RISKS AND THE VEHICLE'S GAUGES AND WARNING LIGHTS

While driving, the driver's risk focus is required to be more immediate (current), focusing on risks such as exceeding the speed limit or suffering mechanical failure. Current risks are monitored by the driver constantly assessing a range of information using the senses of sight, hearing, touch and smell. This is supplemented by the vehicle's dash board where a combination of warning gauges and lights provides real time risk information such as current speed, engine temperature and oil pressure.

RISK INCIDENTS

If no driver action is taken once a gauge or light has indicated a problem, the next stage will usually be the occurrence of a risk incident. A risk incident will almost always involve some negative impact such as financial cost, injury, damage or failure to complete the journey. A record of this incident is usually made in the vehicle's log book.

THE REPAIR SCHEDULE

A repair schedule will be produced by the service mechanic and, in addition to any repairs or improvements we have identified ourselves, forms a list of repairs and improvements that need to be made to the vehicle.

MAINTENANCE CHECKS

A vehicle will contain a maintenance book which sets out the checks that should be carried out on a daily, weekly, monthly or longer basis. This will include checking such things as tyre pressure and oil levels.

These five processes form the key components of managing operational risk in a motor vehicle.

A METHODOLOGY FOR BUSINESS (FIGURE 4.2)

Good practice operational risk management has developed around the concepts and components described previously for managing operational risk in a motor vehicle, albeit with the process names changed.

Figure 4.2   Operational risk management of a business

The elements of a business operational risk management framework are:

The Risk and Control Self Assessment (RCSA). This process is referred to in many ways including 'self assessment', 'control self assessment', 'risk self assessment' and 'risk and control self assessment'. The process for a business is equivalent to the motor vehicle service. RCSA consists of identifying operational risks in the business together with their related controls and assessing the level of risk and perceived effectiveness of those controls. Risk levels are evaluated against pre-determined risk appetite-tolerances and further risk treatment improvements formulated as required. RCSA may also be enhanced using a process called **Scenario Analysis**. This is where specific high consequence risks are analysed by developing plausible but extreme scenarios, then assessing and testing the effectiveness of controls and potential impacts.

Key Risk Indicators (KRIs). KRIs are equivalent to the motor vehicle's gauges and warning lights. The process involves the ongoing collection, tracking, scaling, aggregating and reporting of a range of information that provides an indication as to the current level of various types of operational risk.

Risk Incident Recording and Management. This process is the equivalent of the motor vehicle's log book. Risk incidents, covering all risk types such as occupational health and safety, fraud, security, regulatory breaches and other operational losses, are recorded and managed.

Improvement – Action Point Management and Tracking. This is equivalent to the motor vehicle's repair/improvement schedule where action plans are formulated in response to information derived from risk and control self assessments, key risk indicators, incidents and compliance failures.

Compliance – Internal and External. This process is equivalent to the motor vehicle's maintenance check list. The process documents legislative and regulatory compliance (external compliance) as well as internal policy and control requirements (internal compliance) and seeks to obtain regular attestations from responsible staff as to completion of controls and compliance with external legislation, standards, guidelines and codes.

A COMPLETE FRAMEWORK FOR OPERATIONAL RISK MANAGEMENT

Using the concept of the risk funnel that was introduced in Chapter 1, Figure 4.3 illustrates how the overall operational risk management framework fits together.

First, future potential risks, to which the business is exposed, are many and varied. In Figure 4.3, these risks are represented by the risks at the top of the funnel. Controls are put in place to prevent many of the future potential risks from occurring. Controls are represented in Figure 4.3 by arrows which are pushing the sides of the funnel in and so controlling the number of risks that fall further through the funnel.

Risk and control self assessment is then used to identify and document the future potential risks with their related controls and to assess the level of those risks and the effectiveness of the controls.

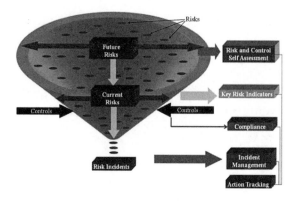

Figure 4.3   A complete operational risk management framework

Secondly, some future potential risks will actually occur, and become current risks, as a result of:

- Unwanted risks being inadequately controlled.

- Small risks that cannot be cost effectively controlled any further.

- Risks with potentially positive outcomes which are deliberately held by the organisation.

The level of current risk is monitored through the key risk indicator (KRI) process. Unwanted risks should be identified quickly and measures put in place to ensure the risk does not lead to an actual risk incident.

Risk incidents will occur. These are represented in Figure 4.3 by risks that have fallen out of the bottom of the risk funnel. These incidents must be monitored, managed and recorded using an incident management process.

The compliance process ensures that controls are being carried out and together with external requirements, are being attested to.

Lastly, control improvements and changes are identified and need recording in an action tracking system to ensure they are actioned.

In the following chapters, each of these components will be analysed in detail to demonstrate how the process is carried out and how each component is used in an overall operational risk management framework.

CONCLUSION

This chapter has outlined the key components of a robust operational risk management process and how they fit together and complement each other. Due to the lifecycle nature of risk, a range of techniques are required to ensure that the risk lifecycle is managed and monitored in the most effective and efficient way.

The following five chapters expand on each component of the framework starting with risk and control self assessment and finishing with risk treatment and action tracking.

⑤ Risk and Control Self Assessment (RCSA)

WHAT IS A RISK AND CONTROL SELF ASSESSMENT?

Risk and control self assessment (RCSA) is the process of identifying, recording and assessing potential risks and related controls. This process is also known by a variety of other names including control self assessment, risk self assessment or, simply, self assessment. Although the fundamental principles of carrying out an RCSA are fairly well accepted, there are a wide range of views as to the best approach at the micro level. Figure 5.1 illustrates that the RCSA process is primarily aimed at identifying and assessing future potential risks rather than current risks or actual risk incidents. The process also identifies and assesses the effectiveness of controls in treating the identified risks.

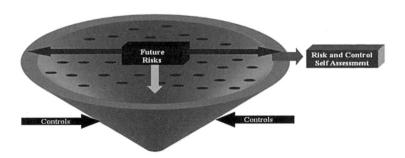

Figure 5.1   Risk and control self assessment

OBJECTIVES OF THE RCSA PROCESS

The RCSA process is primarily designed to:

- Assist the organisation in identifying and documenting all of its material risks together with related controls;

- Assess the level of each risk to enable an evaluation against the risk appetite–tolerance of the organisation;

- Increase risk awareness by the business;

- Encourage the ongoing review of the effectiveness and efficiency of controls and for business to better manage their own risks;

- Increase transparency of risk within business through reporting of the assessment results; and

- Achieve a ranking of the risks to determine which risks require a higher priority and a greater focus.

DESIGNING THE RCSA METHODOLOGY

The detailed design of the RCSA methodology will depend on the nature of the organisation it is being developed for, and the individuals involved in designing it. Some methods may differ fundamentally, others only in the detail. The following guidelines set out a range of aspects to consider when designing the RCSA process.

WHO CARRIES OUT THE ASSESSMENT?

Importantly, the process is a 'self assessment'. As a result, the business line management and staff will be responsible for the completion and maintenance of the RCSA.

HOW OFTEN ARE THE ASSESSMENTS CARRIED OUT AND SUBSEQUENTLY UPDATED?

The frequency of assessment varies by organisation but would usually be carried out no less than annually. On a more frequent basis, the RCSA update may occur semi-annually, quarterly or even monthly. The extent of the assessment update may also differ based on the frequency. For example, an annual update may be in-depth, while more frequent updates may be briefer in nature.

HOW IS THE ASSESSMENT CARRIED OUT?

There is no single approach to carrying out an assessment. Commonly we find the most successful way to complete assessments is to hold workshops with selected managers and staff. These may take multiple days, or at a minimum, a few hours to complete.

Alternatively, assessments may be completed by individual participants on-line and the results compared to determine a consolidated consensus view.

WHAT METHODS ARE USED TO IDENTIFY RISKS?

The first stage of an assessment is to identify the range of risk exposures that the organisation faces. Risk exposures may be identified using either one, or a combination of, a range of methods including:

- Interviewing management and staff of the assessed business;

- Risk questionnaires;

- Review of the history of risk incidents;

- Review of third-party reports including internal and external audit, regulators, rating agencies and consultants;

- Review of external information such as trade and industry journals, newspapers and experiences of other industry participants;

- The use of suggestion boxes and intranet reporting portals;

- Implementation of a 'whistle blowing' process to encourage the reporting of risk issues; and

- Carrying out brainstorming in a workshop environment.

Commonly, we have found the last method to be most effective. This involves workshopping with representatives from the business being assessed, covering both staff and senior management. The workshop may be approached simply, by asking participants directly as to what they see as their risks. This approach can be somewhat daunting and common participant responses may include:

'We don't know where to start'

'How do we know we have all of the important risks?'

'There are so many risks, it is overwhelming'

As a result, a preface to the request for risks is useful, which puts the risk process into context. This preface recognises the fundamental principle that risk is the impact that uncertainty can have on objectives of the business. As a result, the starting point for any risk identification process should be to identify the objectives of the business-activity(ies) being assessed.

We will apply these principles to the example introduced in Chapter 4 relating to the activity of driving a car to work.

1. The first question is: 'What are the objectives of driving a car to work?' The answer may be: 'To arrive at work on time and at a reasonable cost.'

2. Secondly, we recognise that operational risk arises from 'doing things'. We therefore need to articulate the objectives into 'doing' or 'action' statements. Put another way, what are the critical things that must be performed successfully in order for the objectives to be achieved? These are referred to as 'Critical Success Factors (CSFs)'. For the car example: What do we need to do to ensure we arrive at work on time and at a reasonable cost? The answers might be:

- leave home on time
- locate the car
- gain access to the car
- start the car
- drive the car to work at an adequate speed
- park the car close to work
- exit the car and walk to work
- avoid excess costs.

3. Thirdly, we are now in a position to identify risk factors that could impede or prevent the successful completion of the critical success factors. For example, using the first three critical success factors identified in step 2 (Table 5.1):

Table 5.1   Risk identification example

Question	Risk
What could stop you leaving home on time?	You oversleep – the alarm clock does not go off There are unforeseen problem(s) at home with your children You are sick
What could stop you finding your car?	You forgot where you parked it The car has been stolen The car has been towed away by authorities
What could stop you gaining access to the car?	You lost your car keys The car lock malfunctioned

This approach generates a list of risks, sometimes referred to as a risk library or risk universe, which relate directly to the objectives of the activity. When this approach to identifying risk is used, common participant feedback includes such comments as:

'Identifying risks is much easier as I have a reference point (the CSF) to use as a starting point'

'I now feel that at the end of the workshop, we have identified all of the key risks of our business'

'It helps reinforce the importance of risk management to the success of our business'

WHAT ASPECTS OF THE RISK MANAGEMENT PROCESS DO WE CAPTURE AND ASSESS?

Once the risks have been identified, they need to be assessed. This involves the assessment of the likelihood of occurrence and the consequence of occurrence of each risk and the risk reduction impact of related controls. Risks may be assessed at a number of levels as follows:

1. **Inherent Risk**. This is the level of risk prior to assessing the effectiveness of controls. It shows the level of risk (a combination of likelihood and consequence) that exists if all of the current controls were to fail.

2. **Effectiveness of Controls**. This is an assessment as to how effective the controls are in modifying (usually reducing) the risk. The difference between the inherent and residual risk levels represents the effectiveness of current controls.

3. **Residual Risk**. This is the level of risk after assessing the effectiveness of controls. It shows the current level of risk in the business after taking into account the mitigating effects of current controls and treatment methods. Residual risks are sometimes referred to as 'business as usual' (BAU) risks.

4. **Expected Risk**. This is the expected risk level and represents the forecast level of residual risk after taking into account the expected mitigating impacts of the planned control improvements which are yet to be implemented.

5. **Targeted risk**. This is the level of desired risk that is being aimed for. Any gap between expected and targeted risk indicates that additional risk treatments require to be formulated.

These levels are shown diagrammatically as shown in Figure 5.2.

Figure 5.2   Levels of risk assessment

There are differing opinions as to how meaningful and useful some of the risk levels noted above are. The major debate seems to focus on whether it is useful to determine the level of inherent risk or not. The main areas of contention are:

1. What does inherent risk mean?

2. Can inherent risk be determined?

3. Is inherent risk useful as part of a risk assessment process?

WHAT DOES INHERENT RISK MEAN?

There are very few common definitions as to what the term 'inherent risk' means or whether or not to use it. The ISO 31000 standard does not mention 'inherent risk', leaving it to the practitioner to decide on how to deal with it. Inherent risk can be defined as the risk without considering internal controls.

CAN INHERENT RISK BE DETERMINED?

One of the main arguments against the use of inherent risk is the perceived difficult in determining its level. For example, consider physical security risk for a building, that is, the risk that an unauthorised person will access a building and carry out unauthorised and damaging actions. To define inherent risk we ask: 'What is the level of risk before considering controls?' The response is often confusion because:

- The risk assessor has no experience of the risk without controls.

- The risk assessor does not know what is meant by 'no controls'.

Assessing the risk using the likelihood of occurrence and the consequence of occurrence (rating: 1 = low, 5 = high), most responses, if offered, would likely be high–high (5–5).

The difficulty is in determining a consistent inherent risk scenario. For example, does inherent risk mean no security guards, no cctv cameras, no windows, no doors and no walls? This problem can be overcome by defining 'control' and changing the order of the risk assessment.

Defining 'control' as 'a specific action taken by the organisation with the objective of reducing either the likelihood of the risk occurring or the consequence of it occurring' assists the assessor to identify relevant controls. The key factor is that the action taken is 'specific' in reducing the risk. Risk reducing factors that exist but which have not involved a specific action by the business, are not controls under this definition.

The order of the risk assessment steps is then changed. First, the assessor identifies the controls over a risk and records them. Secondly, once this is complete, the inherent risk assessment is performed by asking the question 'What is the level of risk before considering the *identified* controls?'

This overcomes the question of what controls are assumed not to exist or not working. If the assessor has not specifically identified and recorded a control, it is assumed to be present in the inherent risk assessment. These pre-existing controls are often referred to as 'base-line' controls.

In the building security example, we would therefore regard security guards and cctv cameras as controls, but windows and doors would not be considered controls as these would not be the result of a specific management action but instead would be expected to exist in the inherent environment, that is, part of the base-line controls.

This approach, therefore assumes that base-line controls exist in the inherent environment. The inherent risk assessment would be determined based on this assumption.

IS INHERENT RISK USEFUL AS PART OF A RISK ASSESSMENT PROCESS?

Where possible, I am of the view that the determination of inherent risk is useful for the following reasons:

1. It assists in identifying which controls are critical. For example in Figure 5.3, controls over 'perimeter security compromised' are critical in that they reduce the inherent risk score from '20' to '6'. This analysis is then used to select which controls will be subject to periodic attestation as 'key controls'.

2. Internal audit should focus control audits on controls that are critical. In the example above, these are controls that reduce a high inherent risk by a substantial amount to a relatively small residual risk.

3. Scenario analysis for stress testing purposes should be carried out on those risks which have the potential to result in a catastrophic, that is, level 5 consequence. Such a scenario is most likely to occur when a risk with an inherent risk of '5' occurs and the related controls fail. Therefore risks that have an inherent consequence rating of '5' would form the basis for selecting risks that would be subjected to further scenario analysis.

4. Reporting to the board of directors should focus on those risks that have the potential to be catastrophic for the organisation. These are the risks where the inherent consequence is high. (See Figure 5.3.)

The debate over the usefulness of inherent risk will surely continue. The key is to apply the most relevant approach to the type of risk and recognise that not all risks are the same and can be assessed in the same way. Where possible, the determination of inherent risk can be useful in understanding the nature of the risk, the potential worst case scenario and the importance of related controls.

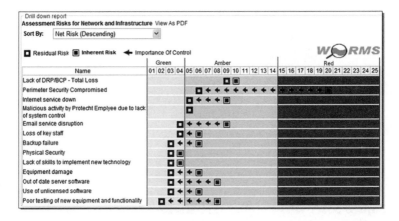

Figure 5.3   Chart showing inherent and residual risk

HOW ARE RISKS ASSESSED?

The assessment of a risk, whether at the inherent, residual, expected or targeted level, requires an assessment of two major components, that of:

1. likelihood of occurrence, and

2. consequence if the risk were to occur.

These are the key elements we defined in Chapter 1 and which can be represented by the probability distribution (see Figure 5.4).

In order to assess the likelihood and consequence for each risk, scales need to be developed for each of these two components ranging from low (low likelihood, low consequence) to high (high likelihood, high consequence).

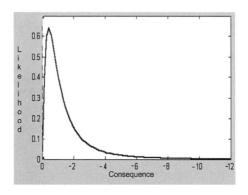

Figure 5.4   Probability distribution for operational risk

DEVELOPING A LIKELIHOOD SCALE

In order to develop a scale for likelihood, the following need
to be determined:

1. How many levels are required in the scale?

2. How will the scale be articulated? Examples include:

    -   percentage chance of occurrence, for example, 30 per
        cent;
    -   frequency of occurrence within a period, for example,
        12 times per year;
    -   qualitative, for example, 'almost never', 'sometimes'
        and so on.

3. What will the scale parameters be for each level? Usually
    the parameters will either be a range, for example, 20 per
    cent to 40 per cent or a single value such as 'almost never'.

An example of likelihood scaling using five levels and the frequency of occurrence as the measure is shown in Table 5.2.

Table 5.2   Likelihood scale example

Level	Scale
5 Very High	More than 52 times per year
4 High	Between 12 and 52 times per year
3 Medium	Between 1 and 12 times per year
2 Low	Between 1 time in 10 years and 1 time per year
1 Very Low	Less than 1 time in 10 years

DEVELOPING A CONSEQUENCE SCALE

In order to develop a scale for consequence, the following need to be determined:

1. How many levels are required in the scale?

2. How will the scale be articulated? Examples include:

  - qualitative, for example, 'high', 'medium', 'low';
  - a range of consequence types – the types used should be based on the objectives of the activity being assessed; for the car case study, we may use:
     a. the number of minutes late for work
     b. the $ cost of the journey.

For business, this will normally include such things as:

    a. monetary cost

    b. opportunity loss

    c. impact on reputation

    d. regulatory breach

    e. customer dissatisfaction.

3. What will the scale parameters be for each level? Usually the parameters will either be a range, for example, $10 million to $20 million or a single value such as 'severe'.

An example consequence scaling using five levels and a range of consequence types would be:

Table 5.3   Consequence scales example

Level	Monetary –Actual and opportunity $ loss	Reputation	Customer satisfaction	Regulatory Breach
5 Very High	Greater than $5 million	Global media coverage	Loss of more than 100 customers	Major breach of critical regulation
4 High	Between $2 and $5 million	National media coverage	Loss of between 40 and 100 customers	Medium breach of critical regulation
3 Medium	Between $500,000 and $2 million	City wide media coverage	Over 1,000 customers unhappy and loss of less than 40 customers	Minor breach of critical regulation
2 Low	Between $50,000 and $500,000	Local media coverage	Between 100 and 1,000 customers unhappy	Major breach of non-critical regulation
1 Very Low	Less than $50,000	Employee coverage	Less than 100 customers unhappy	Minor breach of non-critical regulation

In addition, as illustrated previously in Figure 5.4, for any given risk, there is a range of consequences that could occur, each with a different likelihood of occurrence. As a general observation, for most risks, where the consequence is lower, the likelihood is greater and where the consequence is greater, the likelihood is lower.

When assessing risk as part of the RCSA process, an assessment of the likelihood of occurrence and consequence of occurrence needs to be made for each level of risk required, that is, inherent, residual, expected and targeted.

For example, using our previous car example we could assess the inherent level of 'lost car keys' as shown in Table 5.4.

However, this assessment only identifies one point on the probability distribution and we need to be clear which point we are assessing.

Table 5.4   Inherent risk assessment example

Inherent Risk	Likelihood of occurrence	Consequence of occurrence
Lost car keys	2 (between 1 time per year and once in 10 years)	5 (more than 3 hours late)

Case Study

Assessment. When carrying out a series of facilitated assessments for a client using their internal methodology, it became clear that different business units were assessing the same risk very differently. From my knowledge of the business, I knew that the risks in each business were similar. After further investigation, it became clear that no guidance had been offered to the risk assessors as to whether the likelihood and consequence scaling should be the average expected likelihood and average expected consequence or some kind of extreme or worst case. Some assessors were determining likelihood and consequence levels based on average expectations and others based on a 'worst case scenario'. After clarifying what was expected, the wording was then changed to:

– What is the average number of times you would expect this risk to occur within a 12-month period?

– What is the average expected consequence if the risk were to occur?

This created much more consistency across the assessments. The results could then be compared and aggregated.

Key Point: It is important to specify how the likelihood and consequence should be assessed, whether it is the average or more towards a worst case.

DEVELOPING AN EFFECTIVENESS OF CONTROLS SCALE

In order to develop a scale for the effectiveness of controls, the following need to determined:

1. How many levels are required in the scale?

2. How will the scale be articulated? Examples include:

- percentage level in reduction of the risk, for example, 30 per cent;
- qualitative, for example, 'effective', 'partially effective', 'ineffective'.

3. What will the scale parameters be for each level? Usually the parameters will either be a range, for example, 20 per cent to 40 per cent effective or a single value such as 'partially effective'.

4. An example of likelihood scaling, using five levels and the percentage reduction in risk as the measure, is shown in Table 5.5.

Table 5.5   Effectiveness of controls scale example

Level	Scale
6	80%–100% effective in reducing risk
5	60%–80% effective in reducing risk
4	40%–60% effective in reducing risk
3	20%–40% effective in reducing risk
2	0%–20% effective in reducing risk
1	0% effective in reducing risk

HOW THE DIFFERENT LEVELS OF RISK ARE DETERMINED

If only inherent and residual risk are focussed on, we can use the simple relationship that:

Inherent Risk   IR

Less: The effectiveness of controls   (C)

Equals Residual Risk   **RR**

In order to determine all three components, only two are required to be determined, the third being the balancing figure.

	Likelihood	**Consequence**	**Total**[†]
Inherent Risk	2	5	10
Less:			
The effectiveness of controls	0%	80%	80%
Equals Residual Risk	2	1	2

[†] The total risk is determined by multiplying the likelihood by the consequence.

This analysis can be broken down further to show likelihood and consequence separately. This is illustrated using the 'loss of keys' risk in our vehicle case study.

We will assume that the control is a spare set of keys kept in the house.

RCSA EXAMPLE

Table 5.6 shows the completed RCSA for three example risks identified in the driving to work case study, identifying inherent and residual risk only, and using the methodology and scales set out above.

Table 5.6   Risk Control Self Assessment example

Risk	Treatment methods	Inherent risk. Before considering the effect of treatment methods			Effectiveness of treatment methods		Residual risk. After considering the effect of treatment methods		
		L 1 – low 5 – high	C 1 – low 5 – high	L*C	L 0%– 100%	C 0%– 100%	L 1 – low 5 – high	C 1 – low 5 – high	L*C
1. Oversleep – Alarm clock does not go off	Back-up wake-up call	2	4	8	90%	0%	1	4	4
2. Unforeseen problem(s) at home with children	Child minder on call prearranged flexi days	3	5	15	0%	60%	3	2	6
3. Lost car keys	Spare keys	2	5	10	0%	80%	2	1	2

SCENARIO ANALYSIS

Where the RCSA process focuses on assessing an average consequence, worst case scenarios are not addressed. Average consequence assessments are useful when managing 'business as usual' risks but not in protecting the organisation from a major disaster. Where average assessments are used, it is important to specifically focus on understanding those risks that could produce a major impact on the organisation. The process of focusing on worst case is known as scenario analysis.

In Figure 5.5, the average scenarios implies:

- An average level of consequence when this risk event occurs.

• An average likelihood of this risk event occurring.

However for this risk we can identify any number of other consequences with lower and lower likelihoods of occurrence. Scenario analysis focuses on assessing large consequence situations which may occur very rarely. In Figure 5.5 an 'exceptional' consequence is identified as well as the extreme worst case.

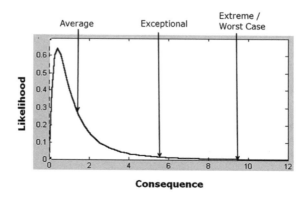

Figure 5.5   Average, exceptional and worst case scenarios

A common process for carrying out scenario analysis is as follows:

1. Risks are identified which are believed to have a potential worst case that is considered to be over a certain pre-determined severe level. These risks may come from a review of the risks in the risk register created from the risk and control self assessment process.

2. For each risk selected, plausible but extreme scenarios are created. These may come from actual past events within the organisation, extreme events that have happened outside of the organisation or theoretical events.

3. The scenario is reviewed and an impact analysis conducted to determine the possible consequence if the risk were to occur.

4. For each scenario a likelihood is assigned.

5. The results of the scenario analyses are reviewed and appropriate action taken where the risk is considered too high.

REPORTING THE RESULTS OF THE RCSA

The results of an RCSA process for a single business unit or area which has been assessed can be reported in a number of ways. The most common way is using a 'heat map' or 'traffic light' report.

Figure 5.6 shows a typical heat map matrix. The likelihood of occurrence is plotted on the vertical access with a rating of 1 – low to 5 – high. The consequence is shown on the horizontal axis from 1 – low to 5 – high. The bottom left quadrants are therefore low likelihood, low consequence risks and shown as a 'green' zone to indicate low risk levels. The top right quadrants are high likelihood and high consequence risks and shown as a 'red' zone to indicate high risk. The amber zone is shown between the green and red zones and contains risks that have a high likelihood and low consequence, low likelihood and high consequence and medium likelihood, medium consequence. This matrix shows the inherent and residual risk level for each risk. The arrow between the inherent and residual risk levels indicates the effect of controls on the risk. Sometimes only residual risk levels are shown.

Where many risks are reported, this two-dimensional report can become busy and difficult to read. A solution is to report a one-dimensional heat map as show in Figure 5.7. The risk 'score' is calculated by multiplying likelihood by consequence. Using a five-level approach for likelihood and consequence, this creates an overall risk score between 1 and 25.

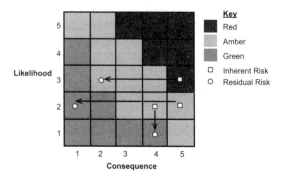

Figure 5.6   RCSA traffic light report example – two-dimensional

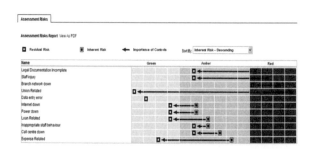

Figure 5.7   RCSA traffic light report example – one-dimensional

92

CONCLUSION

The risk and control self assessment process is a key component of any robust operational risk management framework. It provides a mechanism for gaining engagement with business and a forum for employees – who would not ordinarily stop and consider risk – to think risk. The output of the process includes a better understanding of business operational risks, identification of high risk areas and required improvements, and an overall health check to provide staff, management and boards with transparency of the operational risk aspects of the business.

The next chapter focuses on the process of key risk indicators and how they provide a more dynamic monitoring of operational risk levels across an organisation.

⑥ Key Risk Indicators

DEFINING KEY RISK INDICATORS

Key Risk Indicators (KRIs), as their name suggests, are indicators over the key risks to which the organisation is exposed. They are identifiable pieces of information that act as a proxy or indicator of the current, or potential, level of that key risk.

KRIs primarily track components of a risk story that has already commenced. The occurrence of risk causes and risk events will in most instances produce evidence. This evidence is sometimes referred to as *risk symptoms*, or *risk red flags*. KRIs are designed to identify that evidence, interpret it, and relay it back to management in a meaningful and timely fashion. This will then allow management to take corrective action in order to arrest the risk story so that either no impacts are experienced or the impacts are mitigated.

As highlighted in Figure 6.1, KRIs are focused primarily on identifying and tracking current risk. That is, risk that is happening right now but has not yet necessarily resulted in a negative consequence. A useful way to illustrate the nature of KRIs is shown in Figure 6.2. Risk can be likened to a volume of water passing through the *risk funnel*. KRIs are trying to identify if an excessive flow of water (risk) is passing through the middle section (current risk section) of the funnel. In order to identify and track this, KRIs are placed in positions within the funnel (within the business) similar to a series of 'waterwheels' that react according to the level of current risk passing by.

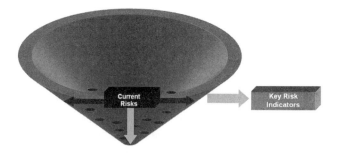

Figure 6.1   Key risk indicators and the risk funnel

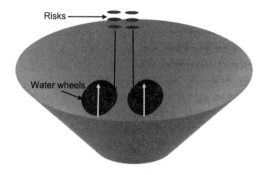

Figure 6.2   How KRIs work

OBJECTIVES OF KRIS

The objectives of using KRIs in operational risk management are many and varied. They may be used to achieve one or more of the following:

1. **Monitor operational risks in as close to a real time mode as possible**. KRIs provide the ability to monitor current operational risk in a timely manner providing management with risk information in as timely a manner as possible.

2. **Detect problems as part of an 'early warning system'**. The identification of current risks in real time provides an early warning system that something is wrong or starting to go wrong. This prompts management to diagnose the problem and attempt to rectify it before further consequences occur.

Case Study

Using KRIs in Caterpillar Trucks. Certain Caterpillar mining trucks use an integrated vehicle system monitoring system (VIMS® Monitoring System). This system is made up of a series of sensors located throughout the vehicle which collect a range of data. This information is able to be remotely transmitted to service engineers who monitor and analyse the data to identify abnormal conditions to prompt further diagnosis and carry out repairs BEFORE they cause extensive damage. This ensures minimum vehicle downtime and maximises production levels. Further information can be found at *www.caterpillar.com*.

3. **Incentivise staff with respect to risk management.** Most staff value ongoing feedback as to their performance. Frequent feedback is rarely given often being left to the annual or semi-annual appraisal reviews. KRIs have the ability to provide frequent and measurable feedback to staff which can act as an effective motivator for workplace performance. Staff realise that their performance is being recognised. This is an example of the cliché 'you get what you measure'.

Case Study

You get what you measure. When implementing an operational risk system with a client, a lack of motivation and engagement by the client's staff was identified as a key risk issue. One client department was responsible for sending monthly reports to their customers by certain cut-off dates and an unacceptably high percentage were being sent late. The introduction of a monthly KRI being 'number of reports sent out past due by date', together with reporting to staff and the recognition of the results by management, soon had the number of overdue reports reduced to zero. The staff became engaged in their monthly KRIs and, with a simple 'well done' from management when the KRIs were all within the acceptable 'green' zone, performance and motivation improved dramatically.

4. **Carry out benchmarking of risk levels across an organisation or against external peers**. The tracking of the same KRIs across multiple similar businesses, or with peer organisations, can highlight star performers and underperformers. An analysis of each often yields best practices by the star performers which can then be

introduced into the underperformers, leading to better control over risk.

Case Study

Benchmarking. A large manufacturing business in the United States were tracking the same KRIs across all of their distribution centres. A comparison of KRIs relating to customer service highlighted that a group of centres around Baltimore were performing much better than the national average. After investigation, it was found that one centre, on the initiative of the centre manager, had identified and purchased an inexpensive piece of software to track the time taken to respond to customer complaints, using this to reduce response times. The manager, through informal discussions with local managers, had introduced this to the local area centres. Suffice to say, the software is now used nationally with a noticeable improvement in customer service.

5. **Provide objective information to manage the business**. KRIs provide objective risk information to management, which is far better than risk information that is passed through informal human channels.

6. **Report risk levels in as timely manner as possible**. KRIs can be collected frequently and allow risk reports to be provided to management on a timely basis. Risk information loses value rapidly the later it is reported after the source date.

7. **Promote the awareness of risk issues across general staff**. The collection, analysis and reporting of KRIs back to a large portion of staff promotes greater risk awareness amongst general staff and provides a focus on what really matters.

8. **Meet regulatory requirements (for certain industries such as banking)**. In some industries, such as banking, KRIs are required to be tracked for certain banks in order to comply with the regulatory requirements of the Basel II prudential regulations.

WHAT CAN KRIs TRACK?

The performance of an organisation can be measured in terms of the degree to which objectives are achieved, compared to the level of risk experienced in pursuit of those objectives. This is often referred to as the 'risk–reward equation'. Key performance indicators (KPIs) tend to be focused on tracking the achievement of objectives (such as the level of sales) while KRIs track the risk component of the risk–reward equation.

In Chapter 5 we introduced the following relationship:

Inherent Risk	IR
Less Controls	(C)
Equals Residual Risk	RR
Less planned control improvements	(PCI)
Equals Expected Risk	ER
Less improvements to be determined	(ID)
Equals Targeted Risk	TR

KRIs can be set up to track any aspect of the above. For example, using the activity of the payment of creditors and the risk of incorrect payments (see Table 6.1)

Table 6.1   Examples of KRIs to track creditor payment errors

Risk component	KRI type	What does it track?	KRI example
Inherent risk	Inherent risk indicator	The level of the inherent risk	Volume of payments
Controls	Control indicator	The performance of the control	Number of outstanding items on the bank reconciliation
Residual risk	Residual risk indicator	The level of residual risk	The number of supplier payment queries
Planned control improvements	Control improvement indicator	The performance over implementing planned improvements	The number of planned improvements past their due by date
Improvements to be determined	Further improvements indicator	The degree to which further planned improvements are required to be formulated	Number of risks where targeted risk is less than expected risk
Targeted risk	Targeted risk indicator	The level of targeted risk	The number of risks where targeted risk is low – medium – high

IDENTIFYING KRIS

The first stage of setting up a successful KRI framework and process is to identify the KRIs that you wish to track. When defining which KRIs to track, the following elements should be considered:

1. **Consider the objective(s) of the KRI**. As discussed earlier in this chapter, there are a variety of objectives which may be pursued with KRIs. Each objective may require a different type of KRI. For example, the use of a KRI for motivating staff, such as the level of processing errors, may well be different from one used for tracking a key organisational risk such as employee dissatisfaction, where staff turnover may be used.

2. **Where the KRI is used to track risk, it should track a 'key risk'**. The starting point will be the organisation's already identified key risks. These key risks may be identified from:

   - the RCSA process
   - actual risk incidents
   - audit – regulatory – consultant reports
   - industry – environment – peer review
   - compliance failure
   - improvement implementation failure.

3. **Avoid tracking too many KRIs**. As a general rule for most business units, 30 KRIs would be considered sufficient. There are, of course, exceptions.

4. **The KRI should ideally have a strong relationship to the risk being tracked**. In order to be a useful KRI, a change in the KRI should be strongly correlated to a change in the tracked risk. Where this relationship is weak, the KRI is less reliable. For example, the level of employee complaints may be considered a strong indicator of poor staff morale, while the level of staff turnover may be considered weaker as there is a wider range of other factors that could cause this.

5. **Leading KRIs are generally considered more valuable than lagging KRIs**. The more leading a KRI is, the more time there is to react and put in measures to fix the problem, prior to a loss incident occurring. Lagging KRIs can be useful where the frequency of the risk is high as although lagging KRIs often track actual risk incidents, those incidents may recur if no action is taken.

6. **The KRI should be easy to collect with minimal burden on the business**. Ideally the KRI information is readily available and just requires collection. If the information is unavailable, a decision needs to made as to whether the extra cost of collection is worthwhile.

ASSESSING THE QUALITY OF KRIS

As a practice aid, I often find it useful to 'score' the quality of KRIs that have been identified. Table 6.2 assesses four key characteristics and uses a scoring of 1 (poor) to 5 (good) for each characteristic. I have used two example KRIs from Table 6.1, relating to creditor payment errors.

Table 6.2   Practice aid for the assessment of KRI quality

KRI	Importance of risk being tracked (5–1)	Strength of relationship to tracked risk (5–1)	Degree of leading rather than lagging (5–1)	Ease of collection (5–1)	Total Score (20–4)
Number of creditor payments	4	1	3	5	13
Number of supplier payment queries	4	5	2	5	16

From this, we would conclude that tracking the number of supplier payment queries is a better KRI than the number of creditor payments.

TYPES OF KRI

We generally recognise three main types of KRI. These are:

1. **Single number KRIs**. An example would be the number of customer complaints.

2. **Composite KRIs**. Composite KRIs consist of two or more single number KRIs combined using an algorithm. An example would be to combine the number of customers with the number of customer complaints to produce a customer complaint ratio (number of customer complaints ÷ number of customers).

3. **Qualitative KRIs**. These are KRIs such as 'Audit rating' which may have qualitative values of high, medium and low.

KRI LIBRARY DATABASE

As KRIs are developed across the business, it is useful to create a KRI library. This library stores all KRIs and can be used by other business units and business areas. In order to create a library, the KRI needs to be 'catalogued'. The following is a list of suggested fields in order to catalogue a KRI.

1. name of KRI

2. description of KRI

3. KRI type (single, composite, qualitative)

4. objective of the KRI

5. what the KRI is tracking

6. the linkage of the KRI to a risk cause(s)

7. the linkage of the KRI to a risk event(s)

8. the linkage of the KRI to a risk effect(s)

9. the linkage of the KRI to control(s).

SETTING UP KRIs READY FOR COLLECTION

Prior to commencing the KRI data collection and reporting process, the KRIs must be 'set up'. This involves:

1. Selecting KRIs that will be collected from the KRI library for each business unit

2. Linking the KRIs to risk categories such as risk causes, risk events, risk effects, controls and processes. This then provides the ability to:

   • Aggregate KRI information at the linked risk, control or process category level;
   • Provide a summary of the category including contributory information from the KRIs; and
   • Produce aggregated dashboard reporting with drill down capability which allows more detailed analysis of aggregated information if required.

3. Assign responsibility for collection of the KRIs to a specific role or person. Specific KRIs that relate to one or very few business units will usually be collected by the specific business unit itself. Generic KRIs (those which are collected across many business units) are usually collected by a central business unit. For example, Human Resources may collect KRIs for employees such as overtime levels.

4. Determine the frequency of collecting the KRI (for example daily, weekly, monthly, quarterly and so on). The minimum frequency will be limited by the frequency of data availability and also be driven by the required frequency of KRI reporting.

5. Determine the frequency and required timeliness of reporting KRIs. Most commonly, KRIs are reported on a monthly basis. Period end reports should be produced and delivered as soon as possible after period end to be of greatest value.

6. In order to be meaningful, KRIs need to be 'scored' into meaningful levels such as high–medium–low or red–amber–green. This is achieved by determining threshold scores which define each level. This process needs to consider:

- The risk appetite–tolerance of the organisation or the business unit involved;
- The number of scoring levels required; and
- The escalation and follow-up action that is expected for KRIs in each level.

Figure 6.3 illustrates a technique I commonly use to determine the thresholds for scoring KRIs using a three-level (red, amber, green) approach.

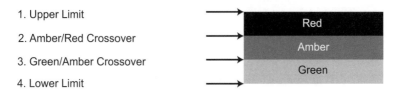

1. Upper Limit

2. Amber/Red Crossover

3. Green/Amber Crossover

4. Lower Limit

Figure 6.3   Setting threshold levels for KRIs

In order to score a KRI using three levels, four thresholds need to be determined as shown in Figure 6.3.

A method to determine these thresholds is to ask the following four questions:

- **To set Level 4**. What is the best possible result you could wish to attain?

- **To set Level 1**. What level would you consider catastrophic?

- **To set Level 3**. What level would you accept as part of normal business without taking any further action to improve?

- **To set Level 2**. What level would you want to take immediate corrective action over?

Case Study

Setting thresholds for a customer complaint KRI. We will assume that we are setting the thresholds for the KRI 'Customer complaint ratio' (number of customer complaints per month ÷ number of customers). We then ask the questions:

- What is the best possible result you could wish to attain? The answer will most likely be 0 per cent. This is our lower level.

- What level would you consider catastrophic (make you want to quit your job)? We may answer 20 per cent. This is our upper level.

- What level would you accept as part of normal business without taking any further action to improve? We may answer 2 per cent. This becomes our green to amber crossover level.

- What level would you want to take immediate corrective action over? We may answer 8 per cent. This becomes our amber to red crossover level as seen in Figure 6.4.

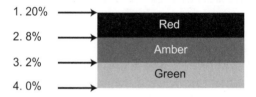

1. 20%
2. 8%
3. 2%
4. 0%

Figure 6.4   Threshold   levels   for   customer complaint ratio

We now have the ability to score the KRI once data is collected.

Case Study

Scoring a KRI. Assume that the KRI score for a given month was 7 per cent. We would normalise the score between 0 and 3, as we have three zones (red, amber, green). The score of 7 per cent would fall in the amber zone, between 2 per cent and 8 per cent. The normalised score would therefore be:

1 + (7%–2%) ÷ (8%–2%) = 1.83. This would result in the KRI being reported as shown in Figure 6.5.

Figure 6.5   Scoring of customer complaint ratio KRI

7. If KRI aggregation is required, determine the weightings for each KRI. Where a larger number of KRIs are collected, reports which show each KRI can become excessive and difficult to read due to information overload. In this situation, it is often useful to aggregate KRIs into summary categories. These categories may be based on the risk cause, risk event, risk effect, control or process. In order to achieve this, we need to assign the KRI to a category and then weight each KRI in that category relative to the others. For example, using the KRI of 'customer complaint ratio' we may assign this to 'customer dissatisfaction' risk. In addition to the KRI 'customer complaint ratio', assume that the following KRIs are also tracked:

- customer satisfaction survey results
- average response time to customer queries.

Table 6.3   KRI weighting and aggregation

KRI	Normalised score	Weighting	Weighted score
Customer complaint ratio	1.83	4	7.32
Customer satisfaction survey results	1.35 (assumed)	5	6.75
Average response time to customer queries	2.16 (assumed)	2	4.32
Total	1.67 (18.39/11)	11	18.39

As shown in Table 6.3, the aggregated score for the 'customer dissatisfaction' risk effect category would therefore be 1.67 and as a result be reported in the amber zone.

KRI COLLECTION PROCESS

Once the KRIs have been defined and set up, the collection process can begin. This requires formal procedures to ensure the process operates effectively and efficiently. The collection process requires:

1. **Notifications and follow up to those responsible for input of the KRI information by the due date**. It is important that all required KRI data is input by the due dates to enable KRI scaling, aggregation and reporting to take place in a timely manner. The most effective solution is automated notifications and follow ups.

2. **A system for collection**. Due to the disparate collection of data by a potentially large number of staff, a software

based collection system is required. Initially a spreadsheet program may suffice but will become constrained fairly quickly as the KRI process matures and expands. Ideally, a specialised software package should be used which provides the required functionality.

3. **Input of KRI data either via a system interface or manually**. Data may be input either manually or automatically via system interfaces (see Figure 6.6).

4. **Quality assurance of KRI data**. Quality assurance procedures to ensure accuracy of data should be carried out prior to processing. This may range from reasonableness checks and exception reporting to manual independent review.

Figure 6.6   Example of KRI manual input

REPORTING

KRIs can be reported in a number of ways. The most common type of reports are as follows.

KRI – PERIOD END TRAFFIC LIGHT REPORTS

These reports show the KRIs for the current month scaled according to their zone (green – amber – red) and position within that zone (see Figure 6.7).

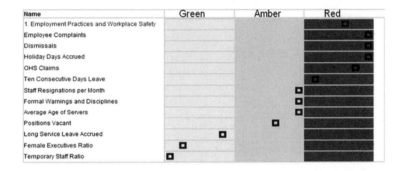

Figure 6.7   KRI traffic light report example

KRI TREND REPORTS

These show the trend of the KRI level over a number of previous periods (see Figure 6.8).

KRI BENCHMARKING REPORTS

These show the same KRI across multiple businesses or business units (see Figure 6.9).

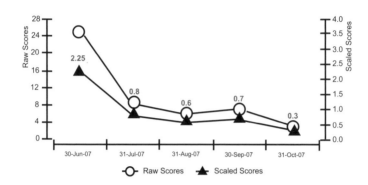

Figure 6.8   KRI trend report example

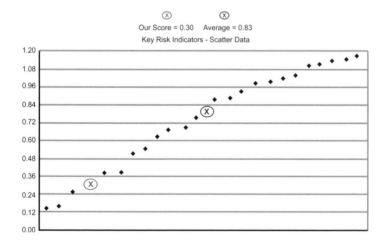

Figure 6.9   KRI benchmarking report example

FOLLOW UP AND ESCALATION

The reporting of scaled KRIs should then lead to follow-up action and escalation based on the KRI score. A KRI escalation and follow-up policy should be developed. This will specify what action is required for KRIs reported in each of the levels, in our example, green, amber and red. An example policy is shown in Table 6.4.

Table 6.4   KRI escalation and action policy

KRI Level	Escalation to:	Action required
Green	No escalation required	No action required. However it is useful to report back to the business unit from a positive perspective.
Amber	Senior management of the business unit and risk management department	Explanation and suggested corrective action provided by the business unit within 21 days of month end.
Red	Chief Risk Officer, Executive Management and Board	Explanation and suggested corrective action provided by the business unit within 10 days of month end.

CONCLUSION

Key risk indicators are a powerful tool in monitoring operational risk in a timely and ongoing fashion. Of all operational risk management tools, KRIs are the most closely aligned to how any engineering processes are risk monitored using dashboards of warning lights and alarm sounds. For example, the cockpit of an aircraft is full of risk indicators and audible alarms monitoring all aspects of the aircraft's operations. The setting up of a KRI process does require substantial effort but when implemented well, the return on that investment is high.

Notwithstanding that an organisation carries out risk and control self assessments and has a robust KRI process, the occurrence of operational risk incidents is inevitable, although hopefully minimised. The next chapter looks at incident management as a process to ensure that all incidents are managed effectively and efficiently so as to minimise any negative impact while also learning from the incident to improve risk control.

(7) Risk Incident Recording and Management

The recording, management and analysis of risk incidents is a critical component of the operational risk management process. The other key components, being risk and control self assessment and key risk indicators, are primarily focused on preventing risk incidents from occurring and if they do occur, to ensure the negative consequence is limited.

Incident management, on the other hand, deals with a risk story that has occurred and has, or will likely lead to, an actual negative consequence. A risk incident therefore occurs once a risk story has reached the risk effect stage. Using the 'risk funnel' concept introduced in Chapter 1, and as illustrated in Figure 7.1, risk incidents can be represented by risk that has passed through, and exited from the bottom of the funnel.

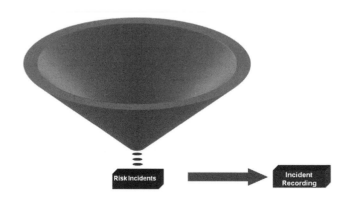

Figure 7.1   Operational risk incidents and the risk funnel

OBJECTIVES OF INCIDENT MANAGEMENT AND RECORDING

The objectives of incident management and recording are to:

1. Minimise the negative consequence of the incident.

2. Ensure we 'learn from our mistakes' and put in place improvements to risk treatments so as to minimise the likelihood of the incident recurring and/or if it does recur, minimise the potential negative consequences.

3. Increase risk awareness across the organisation. The best way for staff to understand risk is from a live case study from within the organisation. Incidents should therefore be used as a risk education and awareness tool.

4. Provide an indication of risk problem areas. This is particularly true where an incident recurs. It is the strongest evidence of the existence of risk.

5. Provide a source of risk identification, especially for risks the organisation was unaware of.

6. Ensure compliance with any external requirements with respect to risk incidents.

7. Use risk incidents as an input into the quantification of operational risk. This topic is covered in Chapter 11.

WHAT IS A RISK INCIDENT?

A risk incident that must be subjected to the incident management process needs to be defined as part of the organisation's risk policies. It may not be worthwhile formally recording and managing small incidents as the cost to manage and record may exceed the benefits derived. The following points need to be considered when formulating this policy:

1. The incident must have actually taken place. It is not something that may happen.

2. In terms of the consequence(s) relating to an incident, which of the following incidents will be captured?

   - Incidents that have caused an actual consequence, for example, a cost that has been incurred.
   - Incidents that have caused a potential consequence, for example, a pending legal claim.

- Incidents that had the potential to cause a consequence but no actual consequence occurred this time. These are normally called 'near misses'.

3. In terms of consequence types, which of the following incidents will be captured?

- Direct consequence
    - financial loss
- Indirect consequence, for example:
    - opportunity loss
    - reputation
    - staff morale
    - regulatory breach
    - customer satisfaction
    - environmental impact.

4. Will incidents with a positive consequence be captured?

5. Will only incidents where the consequence size is above a certain threshold be captured?

6. Are there any regulatory requirements that require certain incident types to be managed in a certain way, recorded and reported? For example, incidents involving human injury require specific management processes in most jurisdictions.

THE INCIDENT MANAGEMENT PROCESS

Not all incident types will require the same actions, escalations, personnel involvement or reporting. As a result, a rigid 'one size fits all' approach to incident recording and management will be inflexible and inefficient. The incident process needs to be tailored according to the incident type. The following factors are most likely to be different according to the nature of the incident:

1. The persons responsible for recording, checking, authorising and reporting the incident.

2. The information that needs to be recorded.

3. The reporting requirements.

In designing an incident management process for a specific incident type, the following needs to be determined:

1. Who will identify the incident and who will be responsible for making the initial record?

2. How should the incident be escalated initially and throughout its life?

3. Who will be responsible for adding and editing information attached to the incident?

4. Who will be responsible for authorising the incident record?

5. Who will be responsible for closing the record?

6. Who will be required to be reported to on the incident and what will those reports contain?

7. What information will be recorded at each stage of the incident management process?

8. Who will be responsible for analysing the incident in relation to risk causes, risk event type, risk effects and failed-weak controls?

9. What, if any, external requirements need to be met with respect to the management process and reporting?

10. Who will be responsible for formulating and implementing control improvements arising from the incident?

WHAT SHOULD BE RECORDED?

The information to be collected for each incident type will vary. However, at a minimum we find it good practice to record:

1. Details of the risk event including any photos, reports, voice recordings and so on;

2. Persons who identified, reported and were involved in the event;

3. Date the incident started, ended, was identified and reported;

4. The incident categorisation based on risk event, risk cause and risk effect categories;

5. Treatments that failed which allowed the incident to occur;

6. Consequences of the event based on type and size, actual or potential;

7. Any recoveries from the incident including insurance;

8. Whether this risk could happen elsewhere in the business and therefore should be notified to those other business units; and

9. Suggested treatment improvements to ensure the incident does not recur.

REPORTING FOR RISK INCIDENTS

The reporting of risk incidents needs to be tailored to the recipient's needs and uses. Reporting may be required for both external and internal purposes. External reporting, such as to a regulatory or government body, needs to meet the specific reporting content, format and timeframes. These external requirements must be built into the incident management process.

Internal reporting needs to consider the use to which the reports will be put, the level of aggregation and summarisation required, and the reporting frequency. This will determine the content and format of the reported information. Reports may be at a more summary level for senior management such as illustrated in Figure 7.2 or at a more detailed level for line management such as illustrated in Figure 7.3.

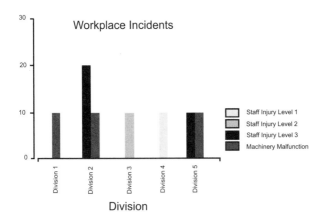

Figure 7.2   Summary   workplace   incidents   report example

Compliance Breach Incidents

Regulation Breached	Incident Detail	Consequence	Financial Loss Amount
Your Business Unit: Branches			
National Privacy Principles	Member details were released to a 3rd party due to incomplete checks on a visitor to the branch.	Major Regulatory Breach	2500
Your Business Unit: Finance and Operational Risk			
APRA	Lack of operational risk management framework rendering APS 310 statement open to challenge by APRA	Major Regulatory Breach	100000
Your Business Unit: Human Resources and Premises			
National Privacy Principles	Personnel file left on desk unattended during lunch break. File disappeared. Found following day in toilets.	Major Regulatory Breach	1000

Figure 7.3   Detailed   compliance   breaches   report example

CONSIDERATIONS TO MAKE INCIDENT MANAGEMENT A SUCCESS

In considering what factors are present in successful incident management and recording processes, the following commonly appear as key attributes:

1. There is one system for all incident types. A common problem with incident management across an organisation is to see multiple incident management systems that have been developed or acquired by different business and interest groups. Each system contains different processes and terminology, with the result that incidents cannot be reported on a consolidated and consistent basis.

2. The process is not overly burdensome.

Case Study

At a client we visited some years back, the comment was made that the incident management system was not being used. On reviewing the system which had been developed internally using a spreadsheet program, it was clear that the amount of information requested and the complexity of the process was way too high. Comments were heard that it took around 75 minutes to input an incident, a sure way of ensuring the system would not be used.

We have found the key to minimising the burden is to allocate the process across a number of people and request only a small amount of tailored information from each person.

3. Encourage and reward staff for reporting risk events. A culture of full disclosure is required so that staff are willing to record incidents, as they occur, without fear of retribution.

4. Provide feedback to staff after reporting risk events. Staff buy-in and engagement is commonly aided by providing the staff who input incident data with feedback as to what happened with the incident.

5. Ensure follow-up action is taken and lessons learned from the incident are used to improve business and control processes.

CONCLUSION

This chapter has reviewed the essential components of an incident management system. In practice, an organisation will often have many different incident management processes and systems, many developed and tailored for specific risk types such as human injury, security breaches and compliance breaches. As part of an operational risk management framework it is important that the incident management processes are consistent and integrated into the overall framework so maximum value can be created from the sharing of information and consolidated reporting.

The next chapter addresses the compliance function as an integrated part of operational risk management.

⑧ Compliance (External and Internal)

Formal and informal compliance functions have operated in most organisations for many years. Compliance as a discipline is well developed, with dedicated education, qualifications, and well established compliance institutes. With the more recent development of operational risk management as a discipline in its own right, the relationship between the two disciplines needed to be defined. It was clear that there should be a strong relationship between compliance and operational risk management. This link arises from the following:

1. The risk of non-compliance with external regulations, rules, standards and laws is a key operational risk for most organisations.

2. Obtaining attestations from responsible personnel for compliance with external requirements, policies, procedures and controls is a key element in operational risk management.

As a result, the compliance function has become a key component of operational risk management.

WHAT IS COMPLIANCE?

Compliance is the process by which an organisation ensures that relevant external and internal requirements such as legislation, rules, guidelines, standards, codes, policies, procedures and controls are complied with. The compliance function assists the business in complying as well as gaining assurance from the business that they have complied.

Many compliance functions have traditionally covered only external requirements (external compliance). The wider definition also takes into account compliance with internal requirements (internal compliance). The wider definition is used here and both internal and external will be covered.

EXTERNAL COMPLIANCE

The objectives of external compliance are to:

1. Provide assurance that the organisation is complying with all material external requirements; and

2. Provide a framework to assist in achieving that compliance.

External compliance may be achieved using a range of approaches. At the more basic level, periodic manual sign off by management of compliance with external requirements is used. More comprehensive approaches involve regular compliance attestations by a wide group of management and staff together with inclusion of non-compliance risk into the ongoing risk and control self assessment process.

The more comprehensive approach will be detailed here.

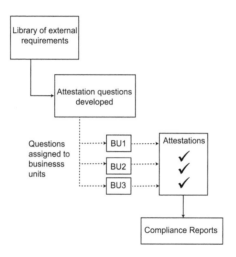

Figure 8.1   Schematic   of   an   external   compliance process

As shown in Figure 8.1, the components required for obtaining attestations are:

1. A library of external compliance requirements. This should cover all major external compliance requirements and needs to be kept up to date as requirements change. These updates should be performed either by an internal department or, as is quite often the case for smaller organisations, by an outsourced specialist legal firm.

2. The development of compliance questions based on the compliance requirements.

3. The assignment of questions to responsible business units, roles and individuals for attestation.

4. The setting of attestation frequency.

5. The notification and follow up of attestations.

6. The reporting of attestation results, escalation and follow-up action.

The assessment of non-compliance risk can be carried out using the risk and control self assessment process covered in Chapter 5. This would be achieved as follows:

1. Risk events consisting of 'non-compliance with xxx requirement' would be identified and populated into the risk event library.

2. The relevant 'non-compliance' risk events would be selected by the business unit(s) for inclusion in their risk library.

3. Controls over the specific non-compliance risk would be identified.

4. The level of inherent risk, the effectiveness of controls and the level of residual risk would be assessed using likelihood and consequence.

5. The resulting risk and control self assessment report would then include 'non-compliance risk' within the overall assessment of risk.

INTERNAL COMPLIANCE

The objectives of internal compliance are to:

1. Provide assurance that all key internal policies, codes, standards and controls are being complied with; and

2. Provide a framework to assist in achieving compliance.

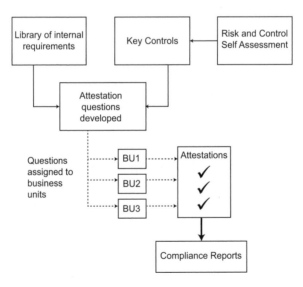

Figure 8.2   Schematic   of   an   internal   compliance process

As shown in Figure 8.2, the key components of an internal compliance process are:

1. A library of internal compliance requirements. This will include all major policies, codes and internal standards of the organisation

2. A library of all key controls. This library would normally be developed and maintained in conjunction with the risk and control self assessment process as this process includes identification of controls and assesses them for effectiveness, thereby allowing identification of the 'key' controls.

3. The development of attestation questions concerning the successful execution of the key controls.

4. The assignment of the attestation questions to relevant business units, and those roles/individuals responsible for the control completion.

5. The setting of attestation frequency.

6. The notification and follow up of attestations.

7. The reporting of attestation results, escalation and follow-up actions.

ADDITIONAL BENEFITS OF THE INTERNAL COMPLIANCE PROCESS

Case Study

Additional benefits of internal compliance. During many of the implementations of operational risk management and compliance frameworks in which I have been involved, the internal compliance process has yielded benefits to the business that I did not initially foresee.

As an example, a large national client implemented a full internal compliance process as part of the implementation of a comprehensive operational risk management framework. As one might expect, the roll out of compliance was not greeted with great warmth from the business. However, over time, feedback from the business showed benefits not initially contemplated. The first was an education process as various business units asked 'how does that control work?' By adding a detailed description to the control attestation question which outlined the purpose of the control and how it should be carried out, the process now provided education on controls to the business. The second common comment was 'what is that control? – we don't do that here!' What became clear was that when business unit management changed, sometimes controls ceased and were not passed on to the new manager. The control attestation process provided an ongoing checklist of which key controls were required in each business independent of a change in management. The internal compliance process had become a substitute controls procedures manual.

REPORTING

Compliance results can be reported in many ways, depending on the purpose and recipient of the report. Reports may range from summary level information for senior management, executive management and board, to more detailed reports for line management.

EXAMPLES OF REPORTS

Compliance Trend Report

This report shows the overall compliance results for the organisation or business area by month. The report shows the percentage of 'Yes' responses, 'No' responses and the level of non-attestation. This report is a high level summary report that would be useful for senior management and board. (See Figure 8.3.)

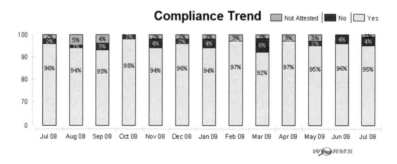

Figure 8.3   Compliance trend report example

Compliance Detail Report

This report provides the detail supporting the summary report. The example provided in Figure 8.4 shows, by business unit, the number of controls and external compliance questions that require attestation, together with the attestation results for the chosen month.

Compliance Summary

Month Ending 30/09/2008

Business Unit	Controls Available	Controls Selected	Questions Assigned	Completed*		Uncompleted or Not Attested*		Change from Prior Month
Australia	84	8	0	0c	0q	8c	0q	↔
Catering	0	0	1	0c	0q	0c	1q	↔
Distressed Fund	10	9	2	8c	2q	1c	0q	↓
Finance and Administration	55	3	0	0c	0q	3c	0q	↑
Indonesia	49	0	0	0c	0q	0c	0q	↔
Landscape Services	0	0	1	0c	0q	0c	1q	↔
Network and Infrastructure	42	0	0	0c	0q	0c	0q	↔
Operations	32	10	0	0c	0q	10c	0q	↑

Figure 8.4   Detailed compliance report example

FOLLOW UP AND ESCALATION

Due to the importance of compliance, follow up and escalation of non-compliance needs to be embedded in policy and supported by a formal process. This would include follow up of failure to complete the compliance attestation. As all compliance requirements will not be of equal importance, the follow up and escalation response should be determined by:

1. The level of importance assigned to the compliance matter.

2. The level of seriousness of the compliance breach.

For example, in terms of compliance importance, each compliance question may be categorised as:

• critical

• non-critical.

In relation to the seriousness of the breach, the following levels may be used:

• major

• medium

• minor.

Once a classification framework for the importance of the compliance question and the level of breach has been determined, a policy for reporting needs to be developed. An example is shown in Table 8.1

Table 8.1   Compliance breach escalation matrix

Importance of compliance question	Breach level			Non-attestation
	Major	**Medium**	**Minor**	
Critical	Immediate reporting to senior executives, Risk Committee, Compliance Committee and Board	Immediate reporting to Chief Risk Officer, Head of Compliance and Compliance Committee	Automatic escalation to Head of Compliance and Risk Officer	Automatic escalation to Chief Risk Officer and Head of Compliance
Non-critical	Automatic escalation to Head of Compliance, line management and Risk Officer	Automatic escalation to line management, Compliance Manager and Risk Officer	Automatic escalation to line management and summary reporting to Risk Officer	Automatic escalation to line management and summary reporting to Risk Officer

CONCLUSION

Compliance as a function, is a critical component of any operational risk management framework. To be most effective, the compliance function should be:

1. An integrated component of operational risk management;

2. Cover both external and internal compliance;

3. Linked directly to the external regulatory requirements;

4. Linked directly with the internal controls that have been identified and assessed as part of the risk and control self assessment process; and

5. Supported by a strong compliance culture which includes formal and well understood escalations and follow-up actions.

If this is achieved, the compliance function will help ensure that external compliance risk is minimised and also that the internal controls on which operational risk management heavily relies, are operated constantly and effectively.

The next chapter addresses risk treatment, formulating and implementing treatment improvements and the tracking of that implementation. This is a process that needs to managed well in order that the risk identification and assessment processes, that have been covered in Chapters 5 to 8, lead to improvements in the way the organisation manages its operational risks.

(9) Risk Treatment, Improvement Implementation and Tracking

One of the key outcomes of an operational risk management process is the development and maintenance of an efficient and effective framework of risk treatments. This framework will cover all processes that modify, usually by reducing, the level of risk.

RISK TREATMENT

Risk treatment is any process or action that has:

- A modifying effect on either, or both, the likelihood and consequence of a risk, or group of risks, or

- Has no modifying effect but allows management to formally accept the risk at its current level.

Risk treatment can therefore:

- maintain

- reduce, or

- increase.

the risk from its current level. Examples for each of these risk modifications are:

MAINTAINING THE RISK AT ITS CURRENT LEVEL

Risk acceptance is a common treatment method. It involves an informed decision to accept and take responsibility for the risk at its current level without taking any further modifying action. Risk acceptance is not the same as doing nothing as there has been no active decision to accept the risk or responsibility taken for retaining it. It is crucial that risk acceptance is supported by informed decision.

Case Study

'Acceptance' vs. 'doing nothing'. An organisation I worked for many years ago had no disaster recovery plan (DRP) in place when I joined as the Head of Risk Management. Naturally, I hastily prepared a business case, with a request for funds, which went to executive management and board for consideration. A response was not forthcoming for some time, so I followed up and received the comment 'This is very expensive – those things [disasters] won't happen to us!' After chasing a further two times and receiving the same response, I added a paragraph to the end of the business case which read:

> 'The executive and board of [XYZ Ltd] fully understand the risks contained in this paper and are willing to accept those risks without any further action.
>
> Signature
>
> (Executive Manager, Board)'

Suffice to say, within 5 days I had the DRP budget approved and proceeded to develop and implement a plan.

A common process of risk acceptance usually involves:

- Automatic acceptance of residual risks that are within the predetermined risk appetite–tolerance of the organisation (refer to Chapter 3).

- Formal acceptance for any residual risk that is outside of the predetermined risk appetite–tolerance. This is usually supported by a 'Risk Acceptance Policy'.

REDUCING THE RISK BELOW ITS CURRENT LEVEL

There are a range of treatment types that result in the risk being reduced below its current level. These include:

- Modifying controls which reduce the likelihood of the risk occurring. These controls are often referred to as 'preventive' controls. For example, the use of security staff prevents unauthorised access to premises.

- Modifying controls which reduce the consequence of the risk if it were to occur. These controls are often referred to as 'reactive' or 'remedial' controls. For example, the use of back-up systems do not prevent the primary system from failing but greatly reduce the consequence if they were to fail.

- Avoiding the risk by:

  - Ceasing, modifying or not commencing the activity that gives rise to the risk. An example would be to automate a manual process. Human error risk may be avoided but new risks, mainly IT risks, would be introduced.

  - Removing the source (hazard) of the risk. For example, dangerous chemicals may be stored on-site. By removing them to an off-site store, the risk has been avoided at the first site. It would however, have created an additional risk at the new site.

- Transferring all, or part, of the risk to a third party. This is usually achieved through risk financing (insurance) or using service level agreements.

INCREASING THE RISK ABOVE ITS CURRENT LEVEL

Risk treatment is often considered only to reduce risk. However, some treatment methods may, or will, increase the level of risk. An increase in operational risk may be deliberate in order to pursue an opportunity or reduce costs, or non-deliberate, arising as a by-product of other risk treatment changes. The following examples help illustrate this:

- Commencing, increasing or changing an activity in order to pursue an opportunity that leads to greater levels of operational risk. An example would be deciding to outsource activities with the objective of cost saving. The level of operational risk may therefore increase due to a new risk exposure to the failure of the outsource supplier.

- Modifying controls which increase the likelihood of the risk occurring. Examples of this would be:

  - Relaxing controls to save cost. It may be that the current level of control is inefficient. That is, the cost of the control is greater than the expected cost of the risk reduction.
  - Relaxing controls to pursue more opportunities and encourage entrepreneurial spirit.

Case Study

Relaxing controls. After completion of an organisational wide risk assessment of a construction company, we held a debrief session with executive management and representatives of the board. As part of the debrief, the divisional managers were requested to comment on what they had gained from the process. As expected, most commented how they were going to improve their controls. However, the manager of a recently acquired division, stated that he planned to RELAX the level of control. He had identified that many development proposals were being rejected, due to stringent controls inherited from the previous owners. As a result, opportunities were being missed. The manager commented that the operational risk management assessment had enabled him to identify, clarify and assess the problem, so that he could now confidently relax particular controls in order to pursue more opportunities.

–   It is often the case that where consequence reducing controls are increased, the likelihood of the risk increases.

Case Study

Controls that increase likelihood. In an earlier life, I pursued the wonderful sport of hang-gliding. A key risk is pilot error. A consequence reducing control for pilot error is the parachute. Sometimes pilots would forget to pack their parachutes. As you may imagine, their focus on cautious flying had to be at a maximum. As a result, the likelihood of pilot error was significantly reduced, though the consequence was greatly increased. When flying with a parachute, pilots are generally much more willing to push the limits, thereby increasing the likelihood of pilot error.

You may relate better to hire car insurance. When you have insurance, you drive the vehicle like a 'hire car'. When you do not take insurance, you drive the vehicle like your own!

Key Point: When you increase controls which reduce the consequence of a risk, be aware that it may produce the side effect of encouraging greater risk taking and thereby increase likelihood.

- Modifying controls which increase the consequence of the risk, if it were to occur.

  - Relaxing controls to save cost. It may be that the current level of control is inefficient. That is, the cost of the control is greater than the expected saving from the reduction in risk. As examples, we may reduce the quality of the disaster recovery plan, in order to save cost. Secondly, we may decide to reduce the level of third-party insurance and self insure instead, again to save on insurance costs. These both lead to an increase in consequence if the risk were to occur.

These various treatment methods, outlined above, can be summarised as in Table 9.1.

Table 9.1   **Summary of operational risk treatment methods**

Treatment method	Impact on the level of risk			Type of control		
	Maintains	Reduces	Increases	Preventive	Detective	Reactive–remedial
1. Risk acceptance	✓					
2. Modifying likelihood reducing controls		✓	✓	✓	✓	
3. Modifying consequence reducing controls		✓	✓		✓	✓
4. Avoiding the risk		✓				
5. Transferring the risk		✓				✓
6. Commencing, increasing, changing the activity to pursue opportunity			✓			

CONTROLS

Controls can be viewed as having the all-encompassing objective of 'modifying' risk. This may involve modifications which both decrease and increase the level of risk. Most people however, take a more restrictive view of controls, focusing only on risk-reducing measures.

In response to many requests for a definition, I developed the following:

> *'A control is a policy, procedure, practice or process specifically put in place in order to reduce the likelihood of the risk occurring and/or the consequence of it occurring.'*

It is important to appreciate that the implementation of risk-reducing controls can result in:

- Exposure to additional operational risks as a result of the new control. For example, automation of a manual process using IT systems creates new exposures to IT related risks that were not present in the manual process.

- The reduction of one risk, but the increase of another. For example, if a lock is placed on a door as a control over unauthorised access, the consequence of fire risk may increase as the locked door may prevent, or slow down, evacuation.

- Only likelihood being reduced while consequence increases, or only consequence being reduced while likelihood increases. The earlier example of hire car insurance, is a case in point.

Controls can be broken down into three main types as follows:

PREVENTIVE

These are controls that seek to prevent the risk from occurring. Examples would include password access controls on systems and the segregation of incompatible duties.

DETECTIVE

These are controls that seek to detect that a risk cause, or risk event, has occurred so that corrective action can be taken prior to an impact occurring. Examples would include the temperature gauge on your vehicle, or in business, a reconciliation of information from different sources in order to identify reconciliation breaks (reconciling differences).

REACTIVE–REMEDIAL

These are controls that seek to mitigate the impact of a risk once it has occurred. Examples would include business continuity – disaster recover planning and insurance.

RELATING CONTROLS TO THE RISK STORY

Figure 9.1 illustrates how the types of control generally relate to risk causes, risk events and risk effects that were covered in Chapter 1.

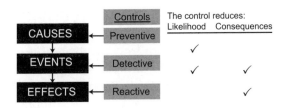

Figure 9.1   Controls and the risk story

1. Preventive controls operate nearer the beginning of the story, usually targeting risk causes. They are aimed at preventing the risk cause and/or some of the early risk events. As a result, these controls are primarily likelihood reducers.

2. Reactive–remedial controls operate near the end of the story once the cause and events have occurred. They are aimed at eliminating or reducing the final effect(s) of the risk. They are primarily consequence reducers.

3. Detective controls operate throughout the risk story but most commonly are focused on detecting whether a risk event has occurred. Depending where in the risk story the detective control operates, it will reduce the consequence of earlier events and reduce the likelihood of later events. For example, a smoke detector is a detective control that reduces the consequence of the electrical fault that has already occurred by providing an alert for early action, but reduces the likelihood of subsequent events such as fire and fire damage.

ASSESSING CONTROL EFFECTIVENESS

Assessing and reporting on control effectiveness is frequently mentioned as an important process in risk management, compliance, assurance and audit. The assessment of control effectiveness is carried out in many ways, incorporating some or all of the 'tests' shown in Figure 9.2.

What?	RCSA	Control attestation	KRIs	Risk Incidents	Audit
1. Control exists	✓				
2. Control is well designed	✓				
3. Control is in operation		✓			
4. Control is performing			✓		
5. Control has not failed				✓	
6. Control is timely	✓	✓			
7. Control is documented	✓				
8. Control is cost effective	✓				
9. Control is audited					✓

Figure 9.2   Assessing control effectiveness

Using the bank reconciliation control as an example, these 'tests' in Figure 9.2 determine whether:

1. **The control exists**. A control cannot be effective unless it actually exists. The identification of controls is normally carried out as part of the risk and control self assessment (RCSA) process. We would ask, 'does a bank reconciliation process exist?' If yes, this control would be documented in the RCSA.

2. **The control is well designed**. This test is usually carried out through an informed, yet subjective review, and involves an assessment of the quality of the control design. A review of what the control does usually provides a reasonable basis for an assessment of its design and is usually undertaken as part of the RCSA. In the example, a bank reconciliation which identifies all discrepancies between the general ledger bank account and the external bank statement would most likely be considered a well designed control.

3. **The control is in operation**. In order for a control to be effective it has to be carried out throughout the period. The control compliance function provides attestation as to operation. The bank reconciliation clerk would be required to attest to the fact that the reconciliation has been completed throughout the attestation period.

4. **The control is performing**. A control may exist, be well designed and be carried out but it may not be performing. For example, if there were 1,000 reconciling items on the bank reconciliation stretching back over a year, it may be considered that this control's performance is poor. This assessment is usually carried out via the collection of key control indicator data, such as the number of outstanding items on the bank reconciliation, as part of the key risk indicator process.

5. **The control has not failed**. If there is evidence that no, or very few, risk incidents to which our control relates have occurred, this gives tangible evidence of the control's effectiveness. The incident management and recording process provides this evidence. Incidents such as long outstanding missed payments and missed receipts would

provide evidence that the bank reconciliation process is not effective.

6. **The control is timely**. A control is most effective when it is carried out as near to the timing of the related activity as possible. A bank reconciliation carried out three weeks after month end is not as effective as one carried out the first day of the new month, as the impact of any errors is likely to be far greater having been left uncorrected for three weeks. Evidence for control timeliness can be obtained as part of the control compliance process, as long as attestations are required soon after the control performance. In addition, the RCSA process may also assess how soon a control is performed as part of the 'design' assessment.

7. **The control is documented**. A control that has some 'after the event' evidence is usually considered more effective than one that has no evidence. For example, a bank reconciliation that is documented as opposed to one that has no evidence, would generally be considered more effective. The RCSA process should consider this factor as part of the control design assessment.

8. **The control is cost effective**. One element of 'effectiveness' is cost-benefit. If the control works well but is extremely expensive it would not be considered as effective as a cheaper control. This assessment requires the calculation and recording of the cost of controls.

9. **The control is audited**. The independent auditing of a control provides further assurance as to its effectiveness. The auditor may carry out both compliance audit work as

well as substantive work involving the re-performance of sample reconciliations.

ASSESSMENT OF AVAILABLE TREATMENTS

Determining a treatment plan for any given risk is a complex process as:

1. There are a wide range of treatment types, as discussed earlier in this chapter, to consider.

2. Within one treatment type there are many different types of specific controls to choose from. For example, there will most likely be multiple controls which reduce the likelihood of a risk.

3. In most situations, a risk will be controlled by more than one treatment method. It is the combination of those methods which together provide the most effective control.

4. Many treatment methods will address more than one risk.

5. Determining the cost-benefit of each method, or a combination of treatment methods, is complex.

SOME RULES TO ASSIST IN TREATMENT ASSESSMENT

1. As a general rule, preventive controls give the best cost-benefit, followed by detective controls and lastly reactive-remedial controls. It is more effective to prevent the risk story from developing rather than having to damage control the impacts after the risk story has fully developed.

As an example, controls over unauthorised access to IT systems causing damage, may have the controls shown in Table 9.2.

Table 9.2   Controls over unauthorised access to IT systems

Control	Control type	Cost-benefit
Password controls	Preventive	Low cost, strong control effectiveness
Intrusion detection software	Detective	Medium cost, medium control effectiveness
Back-up systems	Reactive-Remedial	High cost, medium control effectiveness

2. Identify the range of potential treatment methods and determine:

   - The relative cost-benefit of each; and
   - The extent to which each method modifies risk through impact on likelihood and consequence.

3. Assess the likelihood and consequence of the risk being considered prior to any new or modified treatment methods and then apply the best cost-benefit methods to achieve the targeted risk level.

Figure 9.3 illustrates the example of the risk of 'unauthorised access to IT systems'. The risk has been assessed as: likelihood 5 (high), consequence 5 (high). The targeted risk level of risk is assumed to be: likelihood 1 (low), consequence 2 (low–

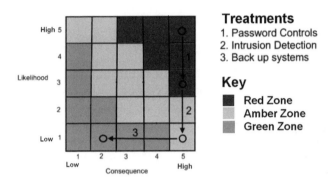

Treatments
1. Password Controls
2. Intrusion Detection
3. Back up systems

Key
■ Red Zone
▨ Amber Zone
▨ Green Zone

Figure 9.3   Example of modifying controls over unauthorised access to IT systems

medium). Applying the identified treatment methods, the preventive control (password control) is selected first as it is aimed closest to the risk cause. This control reduces the likelihood of unauthorised access. The detective controls (intrusion detection) is then applied as it is aimed primarily at identifying that a risk event has occurred, which again reduces the likelihood of unauthorised access causing damage. Lastly we apply the reactive–remedial control (back-up system) which is aimed at reducing the effect of the risk once unauthorised access, which may cause damage, has occurred. The process is like 'reverse snakes and ladders' with the aim of getting as close to the bottom left as efficiently as possible.

ASSESSING THE COST-BENEFIT OF A TREATMENT

In theory, once the process of assessing the cost of a treatment method against the expected benefit is completed, the most cost-effective controls are implemented to the point where the expected benefit of risk reduction equals the cost of the control. That is, if the expected benefit exceeds the cost of control, then the control would be implemented.

In practice, obtaining the required information on expected benefit from risk reduction and cost of control is complex.

First, in order to identify the expected benefit from risk reduction, we need to consider:

1. Our ability to quantify all benefits in monetary terms. What is the monetary value of non-financial impacts such as reduction in reputation risk?

2. Over what time period do we assess the risk reduction benefit. Is it one week, one month, one year, ten years, one hundred years?

3. That controls on their own may not have great risk reduction benefit but when used in conjunction with other controls, they are very powerful.

4. The timing of receiving the benefit of risk reduction. For example, if the risk has a high likelihood and will recur many times in a year, the impact will be felt in the short-term results. If however the risk has a very low likelihood but large consequence, it may not be felt for many years.

5. How the benefit of risk reduction is calculated. Do we simply take the average likelihood × average consequence before and after the proposed control? If this approach is taken, the impact reduction of worst case scenarios is being ignored. Assuming that the average likelihood and average consequence are used together with an assessment period of one year, this average approach is logical as long

as the risk being assessed has a likelihood of at least once per year. For example, assume we have a risk prior to treatment that is assessed as follows:

	Likelihood (L)	Consequence (C)	L × C
Risk prior to treatment	10 per year	$10,000	$100,000
Risk after treatment	2 per year	$7,000	$ 14,000
Risk reduction benefit			$ 86,000

If the proposed treatment had an annualised cost of $50,000 and we have confidence in our numbers, we would rationally implement this control in the absence of a better alternative.

However, where the likelihood is less than once per year, the analysis is less intuitive. Consider:

	Likelihood (L)	Consequence (C)	L × C
Risk prior to treatment	1 in 50 years	$50 million	$1 million
Risk after treatment	1 in 50 years	$10 million	$200,000
Risk reduction benefit			$800,000

Following the earlier logic, if the treatment cost was less than $800,000 p.a. we would implement the treatment and if the cost was greater than $800,000 we would not implement the treatment. The possible implications of this are:

- If the treatment is implemented, a cost of $800,000 would impact the profit and loss account each year; this expense is being incurred for the possibility of saving $40 million, once over the next 50 years.

- If the treatment is not implemented, no treatment expense will be incurred. However, the 1 in 50 years event could occur next year, incurring an additional loss of $40 million compared to implementing the treatment.

Both of these might be hard to justify to the boss!

Secondly, what is the cost of the control? For this we need to consider:

1. Up front, one-off costs. This is often the cost of establishing the control or making capital purchases for the control.

2. Ongoing recurring expense of the control. This usually consists of ongoing maintenance fees and personnel costs relating to the carrying out of the control.

3. Over what period will the cost-benefit assessment be carried out?

   > ***Key Point.*** *Assessing risk treatments, and deciding on which treatments should be implemented, is very complex and cannot be assessed on a pure quantitative basis. Informed judgement is required. I believe it is the role of the operational risk manager to provide management with as much information pertaining to the expected benefit from risk reduction and the expected cost of the controls as possible so that it can*

be collectively evaluated when making the treatment decision.

THE SYSTEM OF INTERNAL CONTROL

The collection of risk treatment methods will make up the internal control system of the organisation and constitutes the first line of defence as outlined in Chapter 1. All activities and processes have some form of internal control system, however basic it may be.

OBJECTIVES OF AN INTERNAL CONTROL SYSTEM

Using the operation of a motor vehicle as an example, the objectives of an internal control system are to:

1. **Allow management to plan, operate and manage.** A vehicle has a range of measures that allow the car to be operated. These measures involve such things as brakes, steering wheel and speedometer. These all provide information and functionality to enable the vehicle to be managed and operated.

2. **Provide management assurance.** The vehicle's gauges and warning lights provide the driver with assurance that everything is operating properly.

3. **Recognition of business problems on a timely basis.** The gauges and warning lights, when activated, provide the driver with timely information that there is a problem so that appropriate action can be taken.

4. **Properly record and account**. A vehicle's speedometer-odometer provides a record of the distance the car has travelled. This must not be tampered with as it provides accountability to the next vehicle purchaser in relation to the vehicle's total distance travelled.

5. **Limit staff**. A risk for any driver is excess speed. Cruise control, where fitted, is aimed at limiting driver input which could lead to excessive speed. In business, this control is represented by limit and delegation structures. These controls can easily be overridden, so it is essential that these limits are being independently reviewed and any breaches escalated for follow-up remedial action.

6. **Ensure objectives are met**. The ultimate goal of any internal control system, is to support the achievement of the organisation's objectives. The vehicle's control system is to ensure the driver and passengers travel from A to B safely, and on time.

TYPES OF CONTROL

As you may imagine, there are hundreds of treatment methods that operate across a typical organisation, each one being tailored to the specific activity and risk. It is an essential task to ensure that those treatment methods are effective in managing the related risk and are cost efficient in delivery.

There are many ways to categorise controls. Each organisation will have different categories. As an example, the following framework categorises controls into 12 categories:

1. **Management**. Controls that relate to management supervision, leadership, governance and guidance. These include governance, policies, frameworks and procedures.

2. **Training**. Controls that relate to the competence of staff.

3. **Compliance**. Controls that ensure external (laws, regulations, codes, standards and guidance) and internal (policies, procedures, codes) requirements are complied with.

4. **Reconciliation**. Controls that are aimed at checking the accuracy and completeness of information from different sources, that should be the same.

5. **Verification**. Controls that are aimed at confirming and checking the accuracy and completeness of information.

6. **Review – Authorisation – Delegation – Limits**. Controls that are aimed at ensuring the integrity of decision making and workforce actions, and controlling the allocation of decision making power.

7. **System**. Controls that are aimed at ensuring the integrity, suitability, availability and correct operation of automated processes.

8. **Segregation of duties**. Controls that relate to the separation of incompatible duties, responsibilities and processes. The purpose is to minimise the potential for an individual to misappropriate the organisation's tangible and intangible assets on their own.

9. **Resource protection and management**. Controls that are aimed at protecting physical assets and managing the risks arising from hazardous assets.

10. **Risk transfer – sharing**. Controls that are aimed at reducing the net consequence of insurable events and transferring some or all of the consequence of the risk to a third party (insurance company).

11. **Legal**. Controls that are aimed at ensuring the enforceability of legal contracts, ensuring the organisation's legal rights are upheld and minimising the occurrence and consequence of legal claims against the organisation.

12. **Business continuity – disaster recovery – crisis plans**. Controls that are aimed at minimising the impact of business disruptions.

Internal audit is not included above, as the audit function is not considered a control. As discussed in Chapters 2 and 3, internal audit is the third line of defence responsible for auditing the internal control system.

FORMULATING AND IMPLEMENTING TREATMENT IMPROVEMENTS

Once changes to existing treatments, or the development of new treatments, have been formulated into improvement action plans and authorised, they must be implemented. Action plans must be managed effectively and efficiently to ensure that all agreed changes are implemented correctly and in a timely fashion.

SOURCES OF IMPROVEMENTS

Improvements to treatment methods may be initiated from a number of sources including from:

1. The Risk and Control Self Assessment (RCSA) process.

2. The key risk indicator (KRI) process, particularly for those KRIs in the amber and red zones.

3. Risk incidents, based on implementing changes to ensure the incident does not happen again.

4. Compliance breaches and non-attestation of external compliance requirements or internal controls.

5. Internal and external audit, regulators, consultants and other third parties.

6. Any other source.

DOCUMENTING IMPROVEMENTS

Improvement action plans should be adequately documented and recorded. This may be effected at a basic level using word processing or spreadsheet. More ideally, specialist action tracking software should be used.

At a minimum, the following information should be recorded:

1. Source of the improvement and the reason why it is required.

2. An outline of the improvement.

3. Resources required to implement the improvement.

4. A cost-benefit analysis. The benefit analysis will provide the 'expected risk' that was discussed in Chapter 5.

5. Approvals for carrying out the improvement.

6. The person responsible for implementing the improvement.

7. The supervisor/manager responsible for ensuring that the change is implemented.

8. The original and revised (if appropriate) due by date(s).

9. An audit trail of updates to the improvement.

AN ACTION TRACKING SYSTEM

The process of formulating and implementing improvements is greatly facilitated by a specialist system that handles and automates all of the steps. Such a system will ideally:

- Form a single repository for all improvements across the organisation regardless of where they were formulated. Often multiple action point systems exist, most commonly with internal audit having a separate system from that used by operational risk management.

- Allow automated notifications, escalations and follow ups. For example:

- Notification to the implementer a certain period prior to the due date;
- Notification to the supervisor that an action has become overdue; and
- Notification to the supervisor that an action has been closed.

REPORTING

Regular reporting on implementation plans is essential for accountability and to ensure that appropriate escalations and follow up occurs. These reports will ordinarily be at a detailed level for line management and staff such as illustrated in Figure 9.4 and at a more summary level for senior management such as illustrated in Figure 9.5.

CONCLUSION

This chapter has covered the concepts of risk treatment and the various methods available to treat risk. In addition, in order to assess levels of residual risk and assess the cost-benefit of treatment methods, a control's effectiveness requires to be assessed. This is not an easy process and in this chapter we have outlined the main elements to assessing control effectiveness. Once improved treatment methods are formulated it is essential that they are implemented in a timely basis. This is the role of an action tracking process.

We have now covered the five key elements of a robust operational risk management process being risk and control self assessment, key risk indicators, incident management, compliance and action tracking. All of these processes involve

Detailed Action Tracking Report

Category	Source Title	Improvement	Action	Assignee	Supervisor	Priority	Status	Original Due Date	Due Date
Control improvement	Failure to follow legal advice received	Lack of formal process of updating and documenting template changes	Put in place procedure and checklist for template amendments. Compliance should review changes prior to implementation			Medium	WIP	30/04/2009	30/04/2009 ⊗

21/02/2009 02:29 - existing process of system change reqest form to be enhanced to include a provision for legal sign off and a history of change
04/02/2009 03:56 - Re-assigned to John Smith - post-workshop for consideration. Issue has been recently raised as part of development of an archive of legal sign off on loan templates.

Figure 9.4 Detailed action tracking report example

Outstanding Actions

Generated: 17/07/2010

Category	Source Title	Action	Assignee	Supervisor	Priority	Status	Original Due Date	Due Date
Demo Demo								
Not set	Router, switch failure	action	CMG Super	David Tattam	Medium	Reopened	13/05/2010	13/05/2010
Internal Audit Finding	Internal Audit	Issue RFP for NII and PVPB model, review available	Entry GBS	Protecht1	High	Assigned	30/06/2010	30/06/2010
Project plan items	Counterparty to trade not credit approved	Consider additional control on credit approval for	A8 Store Entry (Hornsby)	A4 Stores Manager	Low	WIP	30/09/2009	30/06/2010
Internal Audit Finding	Internal Audit	Project manager is currently looking at software s	Entry GBS	Protecht1	Low	Assigned	30/06/2010	30/06/2010
Internal Audit Finding	Internal Audit	Prepare Board submission for NII, PVBP model and s	Entry GBS	Protecht1	High	Assigned	31/07/2010	31/07/2010
Internal Audit	<none>	2. Recommendations The branch staff need to be	Protecht1	CMG Super	High	WIP	31/05/2010	31/08/2010

Figure 9.5 Summary action tracking report example

the recording of a large quantity of data which needs to be analysed, manipulated, aggregated and reported so that interested parties are provided with relevant operational risk information on an ongoing basis. The next chapter looks at the reporting of operational risk.

⑩ Reporting

Risk management is an art form rather than a science. It involves collecting and analysing information to 'paint' a picture about risk, risk being an esoteric concept that relates to potential future and uncertain events. Reporting for operational risk and risk management is therefore, by its nature, a difficult but essential component and end output of operational risk management.

OBJECTIVES OF OPERATIONAL RISK REPORTING

The objectives of operational risk reporting will differ depending on who the recipient is and what role they have in operational risk management. The range of potential objectives will cover such things as providing the recipient with:

1. Assurance over such things as the correct operation of controls or compliance with legislative requirements;

2. Evidence of current operational risk problems such as an increase in the number of customer complaints;

3. Increased levels of risk accountability from the business;

4. Increased awareness of operational risk;

5. Education in operational risk management;

6. Operational risk information with which to make decisions, such as the expected increase in operational risk from proposed outsourcing of a specific function;

7. Operational risk information to be used as the basis of risk-based evaluations on a reward to risk basis; and

8. Operational risk information that can be used as the basis of a risk based incentive scheme.

In terms of the general objectives, the reporting of risk like other business reporting, needs to:

1. Be easily understood.

2. Be clear and concise.

3. Highlight the most important information.

4. Make a clear statement or message.

5. Be timely. The value of any information, not least risk information, loses value rapidly the further away from the 'as at' date it is.

CHALLENGES IN REPORTING OPERATIONAL RISK

The hurdles and complexities facing the preparers of operational risk reports can be substantial. The key impediments to good operational risk reporting are:

1. There is so much available information it is difficult to determine what to leave in and what to leave out.

2. Information across the organisation from diverse sources may be prepared on a different basis so that it is difficult to create meaningful aggregations and comparisons.

3. The information for the reports uses different naming conventions which again makes aggregation difficult.

4. The information being aggregated is at different dates. For example, it is unlikely that all RCSA assessments will be carried out at the same time.

5. The basis for aggregating data may distort the reported message. For example:

    -   Data can be aggregated based on a range of characteristics. Aggregation may be based on risk causes type, risk event type, risk effect type, control type, process type and so on.
    -   Data can be aggregated using several methods. Aggregation may be based on average, aggregate, highest, lowest and so on.
    -   Should data be weighted based on its importance?

6. Operational risk information is sourced from a number of risk tools (RCSA, KRIs, risk incidents, compliance, improvements, quantification). How do we combine them together to form one picture?

RECIPIENTS OF REPORTS

In order to design and implement an operational risk reporting framework and process, the recipients of reports need to be identified and scoped. Recipients will most commonly include both internal and external parties:

1. internal:

   - board
   - senior management
   - line management
   - staff
   - committees.

2. external:

   - regulatory agencies
   - rating agencies
   - statutory agencies
   - shareholders and stock exchanges
   - actual and prospective clients
   - actual and prospective suppliers
   - employees and unions
   - insurance companies.

External reports tend to be highly defined as to content and format and the operational risk management process must be able to produce the required reports by reporting deadlines.

Internal reports tend to cover a wide range of information and required format. Staff reports will most commonly be detailed with information at a granular level, while those for senior management and board will need to be at a higher, more aggregated, summary level.

DESIGNING A REPORTING FRAMEWORK

The design of an operational risk reporting framework needs to take into account a range of considerations:

1. How will the report be delivered? Flexibility is the key as it is likely that different recipients will have different requirements. Delivery methods may include:

   - hard copy
   - electronic:
     - read only format
     - downloadable to read-writable format such as spreadsheet to allow further manipulation and report formatting.
   - on-screen direct tailoring
   - verbal; this is most useful for executives on the run.

2. Will the recipient be given access to the report writing functionality? Many operational risk systems come with their own flexible report writing capability which allows

the recipient to design, tailor and report, as and when required.

3. What information is available? Any given risk report will be limited by the information available. This will be determined by the scope, nature and capabilities of the operational risk management system employed.

4. Report design. In designing operational risk reports, the following basic rules should be considered. These are to:

- maximise the use of icons and pictures: 'a picture paints a thousand words'
- include sufficient charts and tables
- keep the use of writing to a minimum
- keep the report brief.

Case Study

In order to monitor potential engine problems, the driver of a vehicle needs to know engine oil pressure. Of the following two options, how would you expect the driver to have this information reported?

a. A vehicle dashboard with an inbuilt printer. Periodically the printer produces an oil pressure report while the vehicle is in motion with the following format: 'As at dd/mm/yyy the oil pressure in the engine is somewhat rising. This is because the ambient outside temperature is also rising and ....'; or

b. An oil warning light that stays off when everything is OK and lights up when there is a problem.

The latter is an icon, the former a written report.

Case Study

On joining one of my previous employers as Head of Operations, a daily management operations and risk report was presented to me totalling 47 pages. Nearly all of the 47 pages consisted of writing with an almost complete absence of charts, tables, pictures or icons. Next day, I decided to personally take the report to the managing director and made a mental note of where he placed it. The following day I went to see him again and noted that the report had not moved from where it was placed the day before. After some encouragement, he admitted to not reading the daily report but that seeing it gave him some comfort that we must be working hard! He did not read it because he did not understand it. I re-designed the report, condensing it to four pages using icons, tables and charts. I took the new thinner report to the managing director but he was concerned that we were not working as hard! I persevered and talked him through the new report and how to read it. He soon became an avid and knowledgeable reader of the new report, and dare I say, a much more informed managing director.

REPORTING PARAMETERS

The key parameters that drive reporting are:

1. The type of risk information to be shown. For example:

   - Key risk indicators in red only
   - Risk incidents above a certain consequence threshold
   - Risk incidents and results of the latest risk and control self assessment for a specific risk.

2. Whether the information is single or comparison information. Using key risk indicator information as an example, we can report

   - Values at one period end only (single) (see Figure 10.1)
   - This period compared to last period's value and change (relative) (see Figure 10.2)
   - Trend of the indicator over a number of previous periods (relative) (see Figure 10.3)
   - Comparison of the same indicator across a range of activities (relative) (see Figure 10.4).

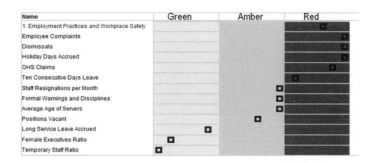

Figure 10.1   KRI month end report example

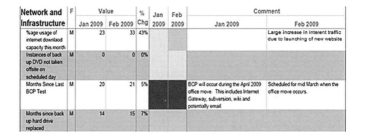

Figure 10.2   KRI period change report example

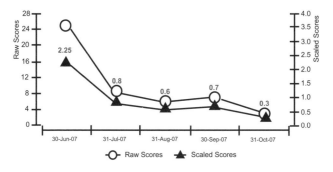

Figure 10.3   KRI trend report example

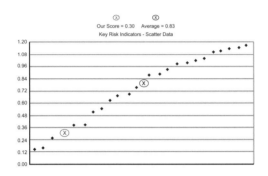

Figure 10.4   KRI comparison report example

3. The 'as at' date or the date range that the information will cover.

4. The scope of the activities being reported. This may be by:

    - geographic region
    - division – business unit
    - process
    - product.

5. The granularity of the information, that is what level of aggregation–summarisation is required?

6. The format of the report. For example:

    - table
    - chart (bar, pie, dial, gauge)
    - descriptive – written.

EXAMPLE OF REPORTS

The number and types of reports that can be produced are almost limitless due to the range of parameter mixes that are possible. A commonly used approach to operational risk reports is the 'dashboard with drill down capability' type reports. These reports cover a wide range of information at a summary level with the ability for the recipient to drill down to a finer level of granularity. Figures 10.5 to 10.10 provide some example reports from a single risk process and aggregated risk process perspective.

SINGLE RISK PROCESS REPORTS

Risk and Control Self Assessment Report

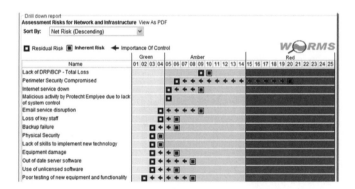

Figure 10.5   Risk and control self assessment report example

Key Risk Indicator Report

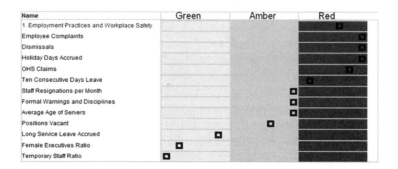

Name	Green	Amber	Red
1. Employment Practices and Workplace Safety			
Employee Complaints			▣
Dismissals			▣
Holiday Days Accrued			▣
OHS Claims			▣
Ten Consecutive Days Leave			▣
Staff Resignations per Month		▣	
Formal Warnings and Disciplines		▣	
Average Age of Servers		▣	
Positions Vacant		▣	
Long Service Leave Accrued		▣	
Female Executives Ratio	▣		
Temporary Staff Ratio	▣		

Figure 10.6   Key risk indicator report example

Risk Incident Report

Figure 10.7   Risk incident report example

Compliance Report

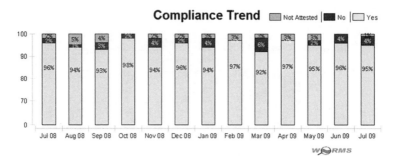

Figure 10.8   Compliance report example

Improvement Tracking Report

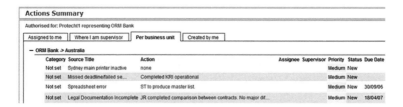

Figure 10.9   Improvement tracking report example

AGGREGATED RISK PROCESS REPORTS

Board Report of Key Risks

TOP 10 RISKS	Total Risk Score		Risk and Control Self Assessment Results as at June 2009 Key: Green 0-4, [illegible] Red 15-26				Key Controls Compliance for month		Key Risk Indicators		Action Plans outstanding		Risk Incidents			
			Average branch score		Worst branch score						Total	Overdue	Month		Year to Date	
Risks			Inherent risk – Before controls	Residual risk – After controls	Inherent risk – Before controls	Residual risk – After controls	Yes %	No %					#	$m	#	$m
1. Potential Breach of Food Safety legislation		■	[illegible]	14	[illegible]	[illegible]	97	[illegible]	■		7	[illegible]	2	2.10	24	13.20
2. Potential Breach of OH&S legislation		■	[illegible]	8	[illegible]	10	92	[illegible]		■	16	[illegible]	4	0.90	32	9.10
3. Excessive controllable expenses		■	12	7	[illegible]	7	100			■	10	[illegible]	2	0.20	12	1.10
4. Excessive inventory holdings		■	[illegible]	6	[illegible]	6	96	[illegible]	■		34	[illegible]	6	4.70	8	5.00
5. Loss of stock		■	[illegible]	6	[illegible]	6	98	[illegible]		■	22	[illegible]	1	1.20	4	3.20
6. Loss of key employee(s)		■	9	5	12	7	N/A[1]		■		3	[illegible]	0	0.00	2	1.10
7. Loss of cash		■	10	4	12	5	97	[illegible]	■		6	[illegible]	2	0.02	3	0.25
8. Loss due to incorrect receipting process		■	9	4	12	5	94	[illegible]		■	16	[illegible]	5	0.43	14	0.92
9. Inadequate product ranging	■		6	4	12	5	N/A[1]			■	12	[illegible]	2	1.60	17	7.50
10. Uncompetitive prices and margins	■		6	3	12	3	97	[illegible]	■		10	[illegible]	1	1.10	3	22.40

Figure 10.10 Board risk report example

TOWARDS THE TRUE DASHBOARD REPORT

As operational risk management and related technology develops, so will the quality of reporting. The key improvements that will be most likely include:

- An increase in the degree of reporting flexibility provided to the user.
- An increase in the speed at which the information is delivered.
- An increase in the range of delivery channels, including moving more towards on-screen, real-time reporting.

These developments will move risk reporting closer to true dashboard reporting.

Case Study

Dashboard reporting. The cockpit of any aircraft provides an excellent example of dashboard based operational risk reporting (see Figure 10.11).

The cockpit provides the pilot with a range of risk information, in real time, presented in a manner that allows them to quickly, efficiently and effectively operate the aircraft. There is maximum use of gauges, warning lights and warning sounds focused on providing real time information on impending or actual problems.

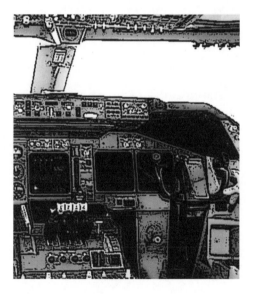

Figure 10.11   Aircraft cockpit

THE FUTURE OF OPERATIONAL RISK REPORTING

A future vision for operational risk reporting in business may therefore be the 'manager's cockpit'. Operational risk information will be provided across the business as close to real time as possible, in a manner that is very easily understood. The information will be focused on providing early warnings of pending operational risk issues as well as providing assurance where all is in order. The information will then be used by the manager to make relevant and timely decisions in a way that ensures operational risk is fully factored into the management decision process.

CONCLUSION

The area of operational risk reporting is in rapid development as operational risk management systems, methodologies and related technology develop. Much work has been achieved in putting in place the processes that acquire large quantities of relevant data. The key is how this data can be turned into meaningful information and disseminated to the relevant people in a timely and easily understood manner.

The next part provides an introduction into the complexities of operational risk quantification.

(11) Approaches to Measuring Operational Risk

The measurement of operational risk is a complex subject. This chapter provides an overview of the quantification of operational risk, the purposes of quantification and how quantification may be performed.

THE NEED FOR QUANTIFICATION

The measurement of operational risk for an activity, business unit, organisation or project may be required for any number of reasons including for:

1. Risk-based pricing in contracts. For example, where project pricing is being carried out, the price needs to include a component for project risk.

2. Risk-based pricing of products and services. Where full risk-based pricing is used, the product or service price

should reflect the relative operational risk inherent in the product or service.

3. Insurance pricing. Insurance companies have long measured the size of the operational risks they are insuring as this forms the basis of policy pricing and liability valuation.

4. Performance measurement using a reward-to-risk-based measurement. For example, the common performance measures of 'risk adjusted return (RAR)', 'risk adjusted return on capital (RAROC)' and 'return on risk adjusted capital (RORAC)' all require the measurement of risk.

5. Regulatory purposes. For example, in the banking industry the Basel II prudential regulations require the quantification of operational risk to ensure that the institution holds sufficient capital to act as a buffer against those risks.

6. Help in understanding and reporting the relative importance of each risk. For example, risks of a larger size should logically be prioritised above smaller risks.

THE FUNDAMENTALS OF OPERATIONAL RISK MEASUREMENT

As described in Chapter 1, operational risk can be broken down into a range of potential consequences together with the expected likelihood of occurrence of those consequences, over a specific future time period. This is illustrated using the probability distribution as shown in Figure 11.1. The probability distribution forms the basis of what is being measured. The components of the measurement process for a single risk are therefore:

1. A future time period to which the measurement will relate.

2. The range of possible consequences over that future time period. The consequences need to be expressed in monetary amounts. This causes problems in terms of quantifying indirect non-financial effects such as reputation or customer satisfaction.

3. The related likelihoods of those consequences occurring during that future time period.

Where a group of operational risks are being collectively measured, correlation between the risks in the group must also be taken into account.

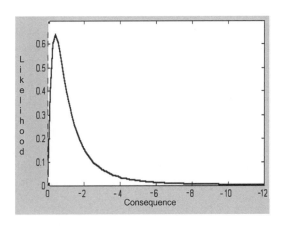

Figure 11.1 Probability distribution for operational risk

MEASURING THE SIZE OF AN INDIVIDUAL RISK

At the simplest level, we can multiply the average expected likelihood of a risk over the future time period, by the average expected consequence. For example, the risk of 'speeding, leading to a speeding fine' over the next 12 months would be calculated as follows:

- the average likelihood of receiving speeding tickets is three

- the average expected fine level is $200

- the average expected cost of speeding fines over a year would therefore be $600 (3 × $200).

We could then use this as a measurement of size of risk in the following statement.

> *There is a 50 per cent chance that we will not incur speeding fine expenses of greater than $600 over the next year.*

One issue with this approach is that, as it uses average likelihood and consequence, it only provides a 50 per cent confidence level that a cost of $600 will not be exceeded over the year. This means that there is a one in two chance that the annual cost will exceed $600. A more prudent approach would be to use a higher level of confidence (see Figure 11.2).

Secondly we have not considered the possible range of fines. For example, a single fine may be $1,000 for speed in excess of 40 kph over the legal limit.

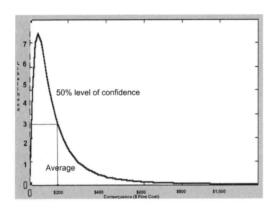

Figure 11.2 **Average risk quantification**

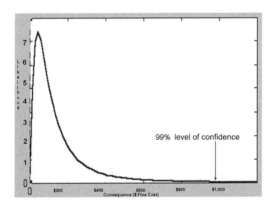

Figure 11.3 **Ninety-nine per cent degree of confidence**

Taking these factors into consideration, a more refined measure would use a higher level of confidence, for example 99 per cent, and take into account the full range of consequences. The risk measure would be the accumulation of all potential losses up to the 99 per cent point.

Assuming that speeding fines can only by $100, $200, $400, $600, $800 or $1,000 the accumulation of potential fines multiplied by their likelihood of occurrence up to the 99th percentile is then calculated. Using Figure 11.3, this would be as shown in Table 11.1.

The accumulation of $1,740 represents the quantity of risk with a 99 per cent level of confidence. This measure can loosely be interpreted as follows.

There is a 99 per cent chance that speeding fine expense will not exceed $1,740 over the next year.

Table 11.1   Calculation   of   99   per   cent   level   of confidence

Consequence (Fine level)	Likelihood (times per year)	%	% cumulative	Consequence x Likelihood	Cumulative
$100	6	59.4%	59.4%	$600	$600
$200	3	29.7%	89.1%	$600	$1,200
$400	0.5	5.0%	94.1%	$200	$1,400
$600	0.3	3.0%	97.0%	$180	$1,580
$800	0.2	2.0%	99.0%	$160	$1,740
$1,000	0.1	1.0%	100.0%	$100	$1,840
TOTAL	10.1	100.0%		$1,840	

As we increase the complexity of the quantification, the degree of independence between the different consequence levels also needs to be considered. For example, the above analysis assumes that all speeding events are independent. In reality, receiving a speeding fine would most likely reduce the likelihood of receiving a second speeding fine, and so on, as the driver reacts to the fines by slowing down. These considerations fall beyond the scope of this introductory text.

MEASURING THE AGGREGATE SIZE OF MULTIPLE RISKS

Developing operational risk measurement from measuring single risks, to measuring a group of different risks, necessitates consideration of the degree of correlation between the different risks. For example, the occurrence of one risk may increase the likelihood of the other risk occurring. This is positive correlation. Conversely, the occurrence of one risk may reduce the chances or preclude the other risk occurring. This is negative correlation. Lastly, there may be no relationship between the two risks. This is zero correlation.

The correlation effect between risks is substantial. As an example, assuming 2 risks were measured individually, using standard deviation as the measure, at $45,000 and $27,000 respectively:

- Where the correlation between the risks is +1, the aggregate of the two risks would be their sum, being $72,000.[†]

- Where the correlation between the risks is +0.5 the aggregate of the two risks is $63,000.[†]

- Where the correlation between the risks is 0, the aggregate of the two risks is $52,500.[†]

Note: [†] The level of risk after incorporating a correlation effect is calculated as $Risk = \sqrt{(Risk1^2 + Risk2^2 + 2 \times Risk1 \times Risk2 \times Correlation)}$.

LOSS DISTRIBUTION APPROACHES

Measurement methods based on the probability distribution, as described previously, are known as 'loss distribution approaches' and are widely used as the basis of operational risk measurement. However, there are many approaches to deriving the loss distribution and other key components, which gives rise to a wide range of quantification methods.

DATA INPUTS TO THE MODEL

The derivation may be based on a wide range of inputs such as:

1. Historical risk incidents of the organisation itself. This is referred to as 'internal data' (covered in Chapter 7).

2. Historical risk incidents of peers and third parties. This is referred to as 'external data'.

3. Scenario analysis (covered in Chapter 5).

4. Key risk indicators (covered in Chapter 6).

5. Risk and control self assessment (covered in Chapter 5).

METHODS TO COMPUTE THE LOSS DISTRIBUTION

Once the data sources are determined, the computation of the loss distribution can be carried out using a number, or combination, of techniques including:

1. **Historical**. Basing the distribution on risk incidents (consequences and frequencies) that have occurred previously.

2. **Statistical**. Using pre-determined distributions, such as 'normal', log-normal', 'exponential', 'poisson', 'weibull' and so on, as a proxy for the shape of the loss distribution.

3. **Simulation**. Using Monte Carlo simulation techniques to simulate a large number (30,000–200,000 is not uncommon) of consequences together with their frequency of occurrence.

4. **Other techniques**. As operational risk measurement matures, there are an increasing number of new approaches and variations to existing approaches based on mathematical, statistical and artificial intelligence techniques that are being applied. These are the subject of more specialist texts.

QUALITATIVE ADJUSTMENTS

As the majority of techniques used to determine the loss distribution are based on historical data, the loss distribution may not adequately reflect the current and future operational risk environment. For example, an organisation may have had poor operational risk control for many years, yet over the last year, has invested heavily in implementing control improvements. A quantification technique which is therefore based on historical internal data will most likely overstate the level of operational risk, as it will not reflect the recent improvements in the control environment. As a result, indicators of the current control and risk environment, such as key risk indicators and the results of risk and control self assessments, may be used to adjust/scale the loss distribution. These adjustments, to better reflect the current control and risk environment, are generally referred to as 'qualitative adjustments'. For example, if the 'number of transactions' is used as an indicator and that number has doubled comparing the current year to the average of the historical data period, the risk quantification using historical loss data may be scaled up by a factor of two, assuming that there is a '+1' correlation between transaction numbers and operational risk.

RISK CAPITAL AND CAPITAL ADEQUACY

'Risk capital' is often used as a reference to the quantity of risk. The reason for this is that the final buffer for most organisations against the negative financial impact of risk, is the organisation's capital. Once that capital is used up, the organisation is technically insolvent.

Some industries, particularly the financial services industries, often use the concept of 'capital adequacy' to measure the degree to which the organisation's actual capital exceeds, or falls short of, the level of risk.

THE PURPOSE OF RISK CAPITAL AND CAPITAL ADEQUACY

The calculation of the amount of capital required to 'support' the level of risk an organisation faces may be used in a number of ways as follows:

1. To calculate 'capital adequacy' as a means of demonstrating financial stability and robustness. For example, in the banking industry, industry regulators require the calculation of capital adequacy ratios and the meeting of minimum capital ratios.

2. To allocate the capital to each business area so that performance may be measured as a percentage return on risk capital. The measure 'return on risk adjusted capital' (RORAC) is an example of such a measure.

3. To be used as a factor in product and service pricing to reflect the risk inherent in the product or service. We would expect a service that exposes the organisation to higher levels of operational risk to be priced at a premium to a similar service that contains only small levels of operational risk.

Case Study

An illustration of risk capital and capital adequacy. In training courses, I often use the following analogy to illustrate risk capital and capital adequacy. I ask participants to imagine that they are going on holiday for five weeks to Africa. One week in Johannesburg sightseeing, followed by a flight to Nairobi, Kenya, to join a four-wheel drive safari in the Masai Mara and Serengeti for two weeks. A visit to Tanzania then involves one week living with a bush tribe, followed by one week canoeing down the

Zambezi river observing hippopotami from a dug-out canoe. Assuming all preparations that would normally be expected, including travel insurance, inoculations and so on, have been made, I ask the participants the following question:

> 'Determine an amount of money where you would be 99 per cent confident that during the holiday, any unforeseen events (operational risk events) would not cost you more than the amount. Put another way, if you went on this holiday 100 times, you would expect that only once the actual cost would exceed the figure you determine. Events that are non-financial should be considered in financial terms based on what it would cost to rectify. For example, the loss of your camera and photos at the end of your holiday would require a new camera and revisiting all the places to retake the pictures less any insurance recovery'.

If we assume the figure is USD 25,000, this is the quantity of operational risk on this holiday using a 99 per cent degree of confidence. We can then compare this to the actual capital that you have, being your net wealth. This is capital adequacy. For example, assuming that personal net wealth is USD 40,000, we can calculate capital adequacy by:

Capital ÷ Risk.

If this ratio exceeds 1, we are capital adequate and if less than 1, we are capital inadequate.

Applying this to the numbers above, we have

Capital (USD 40,000) ÷ Risk (USD 25,000) = 1.6

This gives us assurance that there is a 99 per cent chance that anything unforeseen occurring on this holiday will not use up all of our capital and bankrupt us.

ALLOCATING AND USING RISK CAPITAL IN THE BUSINESS

Risk based performance measurement is an important management tool to ensure that both performance and related risk are both being adequately managed. It allows the organisation to focus on activities which provide the best performance for the risk being taken. This measure is often referred to as the 'risk–reward ratio'.

Using financial measures of performance, risk-based performance is commonly measured using one of three main approaches:

1. **Risk Adjusted Return (RAR).** This method involves calculating a notional financial charge based on the level of risk capital used in the business. For example, if the risk capital was calculated as $50 million and the organisation's cost of capital is 10 per cent, the annual risk capital charge would be $5 million ($50 million × 10 per cent). This notional charge is made against the business unit's profit to arrive at a risk adjusted return. Assuming the unadjusted annual profit was $12 million, the RAR would be $7 million ($12 million – $5 million).

2. **Return on Risk Adjusted Capital (RORAC).** This method uses the business's unadjusted profit and divides by the amount of risk capital. For example, if the same

business unit's annual unadjusted profit was $12 million, the RORAC would be: $12 million ÷ $50 million = 24 per cent.

3. **Risk Adjusted Return on Capital (RAROC)**. This method takes measurement method 1 (RAR) and divides this measure by the business's accounting capital. For example, if the accounting capital was $60 million, the RAROC would be: $7 million ÷ $60 million = 11.67 per cent.

CONCLUSION

Although many organisations will not formally quantify levels of operational risk, some industries such as banking, require quantification to take place as part of ensuring an organisation has sufficient capital to support its risks. Other industries such as insurance require quantification for premium pricing, while others quantify to be able to use in performance measurement. At the present time, operational risk quantification is largely the domain of the quantitative analyst. However as quantification methods develop and are better understood, the quantification of operational risk is likely to become more widespread and more widely used in risk management decisions.

The next and final chapter takes a practical look at what is required to make operational risk management a success.

PART 3

Making Operational Risk Management Work

(12) The Key to Achieving Operational Risk Management Success

Many risk managers find it difficult to obtain the required level of buy-in and investment from the organisation. This lack of engagement may be organisation-wide or from only certain business areas and levels. In these organisations, operational risk management is often seen as:

'audit with another name'

'just another overhead'

'another layer of bureaucracy'

'more work for me'

This attitude and perception creates strong resistance from the business to fully embrace and implement operational risk management. This chapter seeks to assist the manager who is facing this resistance by analysing what operational risk management success is and how it can best be achieved through engaging the business from a 'benefit to you' rather than a 'hassle for you' perspective.

WHAT IS OPERATIONAL RISK MANAGEMENT SUCCESS AND HOW CAN IT BE MEASURED?

As for any project or function, the measurement of success firstly requires the identification of objectives. For operational risk management, the common objectives were reviewed in Chapter 1 and included:

1. Reducing avoidable losses.

2. Reducing insurance costs.

3. Protecting and enhancing reputation.

4. Protecting and/or improving credit rating.

5. Improving risk and control culture.

6. Improving awareness, objectivity, transparency of, and accountability for, risk.

7. Improving the efficiency and effectiveness of controls and processes.

8. Providing greater levels of assurance to management.

9. Assisting management in meeting external requirements.

10. Identifying opportunities relating to risk.

Ideally metrics over the objectives should be put in place that capture the contribution that operational risk management has had on each objective. The difficulties with achieving this are:

1. The objectives may be subjective and difficult to measure, such as protecting and enhancing reputation.

2. The causal effect between operational risk management and the objectives may be difficult to prove because of other contributing factors and time lag between the effort and the result.

3. The successes of operational risk management are often what does not happen rather than what does. It is difficult to prove that a risk did not happen due to what was done rather than it not happening due to chance.

WAYS TO MEASURE SUCCESS

The following are a collection of ways that we have used to attempt to measure success with a range of clients. Not all will be appropriate in every situation.

1. Carrying out surveys with staff, management, board and third parties and tracking the responses over time. The surveys may include such things as satisfaction, risk and

control culture, morale, level of risk awareness and level of assurance provided.

Case Study

Customer satisfaction. A service-oriented company had a poor customer satisfaction history and as part of the operational risk management implementation identified this as a key risk. They employed an independent agency to carry out customer satisfaction surveys prior to implementation of the risk process and at periodic intervals since. There was an undeniable and clear trend of improvement over the period which was attributed to the focus on risk management.

2. Attaching key risk indicators to success metrics. When we looked back over a number of years with many of our clients, it was clear that trends in key risk indicators had improved dramatically over the time since operational risk management was first implemented. I find this a particularly useful measure which is easily available if a comprehensive key risk indicator process is in place.

3. Tracking the level of risk related incidents and losses. Care has to be taken with this metric as on initial implementation of the risk process, reported incidents tend to rise. This is not because the number of risk incidents are rising, but because more risk incidents are being recorded. Once the incident management process has become mature and there is comfort that all reportable incidents are being recorded, monitoring the trend in the number and severity of incidents, will provide strong feedback as to the ultimate success of the risk management process.

4. The operational risk management efforts and results should be used when negotiating insurance premiums. The risk information should be used directly in negotiations to demonstrate the organisation's commitment to risk management and also provide greater transparency for the insurer. It is usually fairly easy to identify any premium cost savings due to the quality of risk processes.

5. Direct discussion with third parties such as rating agencies, regulators and external audit. These discussions and feedback should cover how each party have assessed the change in operational risk management and how that change has had a direct effect on any credit rating, regulatory stance or audit fee.

6. Use of industry and peer benchmarking of risk related information, if available. The common difficulties with benchmarking are the lack of willingness of peers to share information and the difficulty in ensuring the data being compared is on a similar basis.

GENERAL MEASURES OF SUCCESS

In discussions with various risk managers on the topic of the 'value add' and 'success' of operational risk management, a number of general success measures have been mentioned. These include:

1. The degree to which operational risk management is mentioned, especially as a stand-alone discipline, separate from day-to day-management. One particular risk manager had as a key objective 'to develop operational risk management to the stage where it is no longer talked about as a separate function'. It should be something

that everyone does implicitly as part of their day-to-day activities.

Case Study

Crossing the road. When you walk up to a road in order to cross it, what do you do? Do you:

- Find and read your risk management policy.

- Formally identify all the risks you face including car risk, weather risk, uneven road surface risk and so on.

- Identify all controls over each risk.

- Assess each risk according to likelihood and consequence.

- Assess whether the residual risk is within your risk tolerance.

- Decide only then whether or not to cross the road.

or do you simply look around, quickly absorb all relevant information and decide when to cross without even formally thinking about the word 'RISK'.

This level of integration into day-to-day activities is what this particular risk manager is trying to achieve.

2. The degree to which operational risk management has changed staff and management behaviour, for the better.

Case Study

Changing staff behaviour. During one of my previous roles as head of operations at an international bank, the settlements manager walked into my office one day and showed me a particularly complex deal which had just been completed. 'How do I process this?' she said. We had not prepared for such a deal and had no specialist product system. After having to process 144 separate trades in order to record the deal in the general ledger and having made errors on five of them we reflected back at the cost of the risk brought by that trade. This included such things as failed settlements and overdraft interest – a figure of some $50,000. On asking the dealer how much profit he had made, $12,000 was the response. So the net position was a $38,000 loss to the bank – not a satisfactory situation! When I requested that he no longer execute such trades I was curtly told 'these trades are very profitable for me'.

The issue was that no account was being taken of the substantial operational risk to which this deal exposed the bank. After some rudimentary calculations, I gained approval to impose an internal 'charge' on each deal type to take into account the different levels of operational risk. This deal would have received around a $30,000 operational risk charge. Once this charge was imposed on the dealer, we never saw one of these deals being done again. This recognition of operational risk, and making the dealer accountable for it, changed the dealer decision making for the better. We were no longer executing loss making deals.

THE HURDLES TO SUCCESS AND HOW TO OVERCOME THEM

Achieving success in operational risk management is not easy. The main reasons for this, together with suggestions of how to overcome or limit these problems are shown in Table 12.1.

Table 12.1 Overcoming hurdles to success

Hurdle	Solutions
In its modern form, operational risk management is a young discipline. Developments in thinking, methodologies, software and practices are rapid. Something you attempt today may be obsolete thinking tomorrow.	• Create a blueprint of where you want your operational risk management to go, not necessarily limited by what is currently available. • Keep up to date with industry developments. • Be open to new ideas. • Be flexible to changes in your approach as you go. • Consider the newer and smaller consulting and software providers. They are often quicker to change and develop new ideas.
Due to the relative immaturity of operational risk management as a discipline, there is a general lack of risk knowledge across many organisations.	• Education, education, education! Educate all levels of the organisation from board to junior staff in what operational risk is, how it can be managed, and the benefits of good management. I refer to this as 'preparing the ground'. This is an essential first stage of any implementation.
It is a daunting project due to its sheer size in time, effort, cost and uncertainty of outcomes.	• Prepare a 'blueprint' document of what you want to achieve in operational risk management. • Consider 'proof of concept' pilot implementations in one business unit before an organisation-wide roll-out is attempted. • Research organisations who have gone before and learn from their successes and failures. • Consider the wide range of potential solutions that are available and select carefully. In particular, there are many comprehensive web-based (cloud-ware) solutions available which can provide an excellent solution at minimal cost.

Table 12.1 *Continued*

The scope and range of operational risk management is vast. It encapsulates an almost endless array of risks which are constantly changing. It impacts and is influenced by everything we do and everyone we have a relationship with – staff, suppliers, customers, regulators, insurers and so on.	• Employ a decentralised approach to operational risk management, ensuring as many people as possible are involved in some aspect, whether it be a full risk assessment or a simple attestation of a control. • Employ the '80:20' rule. That is, 80 per cent of total risk will arise from only 20 per cent of the risks. • Ensure your methodology will easily filter out what really matters. • Ensure reporting is comprehensive and relays the key issues and matters efficiently and effectively.
A common complaint with risk managers is 'I don't have enough staff!'	• Every staff member should be considered an operational risk management resource. Operational risk management is the responsibility of everyone and should be carried out by everyone (almost!). If just 5 minutes per month is harnessed from every employee, there should be more than enough human resource.
The quantity of information collected and analysed is substantial. This, together with the number of risk management processes (RCSA, KRIs, risk incidents, compliance, improvements and quantification), can lead to analysis paralysis, information overload, confused and inconsistent reporting and the inability to sort the important from the unimportant.	• Ensure that you get the right system. The system you employ must be able to gather and analyse all of the required information effectively and efficiently. Meaningful aggregated and summarised reports, that management can easily interpret and act upon, must be obtainable on a timely basis.
It requires the buy-in and involvement of a large group of individuals within an organisation from board, through management, to staff. Successful risk management requires input, effort and acceptance by all of these levels. This can be hard to achieve.	• 'Prepare the ground' through education • Find out 'what's in it for them' and deliver it. In the next section of this chapter, some anecdotes to help in achieving this are discussed • Gain sponsorship from the board and senior management first • Focus on the 'doubters' and attempt to 'convert' them.

Table 12.1   *Continued*

There are a vast array of consultants, advisors, trainers and software providers. To the prospective purchaser, knowing who to work with, and what to look for can be a formidable task. As a provider of risk management software, we are constantly amazed at the number of so called 'operational risk management' systems in the market globally.	• Choose wisely! • Assess the individual you will work with rather than the firm. That is who you will be dealing with. • Obtain, check and talk with reference sites. • Assess the degree to which the firm is practical and hands on. We find the best consultants and software providers have 'been there and done that'. This means they have practical management experience and know what it is like to get staff to buy-in to something and make it work. • Ignore the name of the software and the glossy wild claims of what it can do and see what it actually does. • The smaller provider may end up being a better fit with your organisation as you will be a much more important client for them than for a larger provider.
The cost of operational risk management is not insignificant. Sufficient resources need to be dedicated for success to be achieved.	• For essentially the same operational risk management process and outputs, we have observed a wide range of cost levels. Implementing a successful risk function may not be as expensive as you first think • Consider periodic licence fees for software rather than up-front fixed costs. This reduces your investment risk and also keeps the provider honest! They will not get paid if they do not deliver! • Consider a 'proof of concept' pilot implementation first. This minimises your investment risk, you see what the software can do first hand, and you obtain experience of working with the supplier.

Table 12.1   *Concluded*

With many organisations, there is a substantial amount of legacy, history and 'baggage' which can hinder true success. This is particularly true in the traditional risk specialist areas such as health and safety, legal, compliance, insurance, internal audit, and so on, who have often developed or adopted their own methodology and systems. In order to achieve true risk management success, these specialist areas need to become coordinated and consistent, which may require a change in methodology and systems. This can be difficult to achieve.	• Refer to the case study below under the 'Hurdles to integration' section. • Consider the feasibility and effectiveness of interfacing between existing legacy systems and the overall operational risk management system. If successful, this can keep all parties happy.
Operational risk management can sometimes be considered as a 'project' rather than a 'process'.	• Operational risk management is a process and must be embedded as such across the business. In order to assess this, I often use the hypothetical scenario 'if all operational risk management staff were to go on extended leave for 12 months, what would be the state of operational risk management on their return?' If it has maintained and improved through its own momentum, you have a process. If it has declined and maybe even ceased, you had a project.

OBTAINING THE BUY-IN AND SPONSORSHIP OF BOARD, MANAGEMENT AND STAFF FOR OPERATIONAL RISK

This hurdle is often mentioned as the largest amongst those attempting to implement operational risk management in a business. ISO 31000: 2009 *Risk Management: Principles and guidelines*, identifies 'Mandate and Commitment' as the first stage of a risk framework. Successful ongoing risk management requires strong and sustained commitment by management as well as planning to achieve commitment at all levels. I have heard the Australian banking regulator (Australian Prudential Regulation Authority) using the invented, but very apt, word 'embeddedness' to reflect the degree to which operational risk management has been embedded in the business. Embedding risk management can only be achieved with the buy-in, sponsorship and commitment of all levels of the organisation. So how do we achieve buy-in?

Case Study

Some years ago, I listened to a short dinner speech by the head of operational risk management at a major US company. He opened by saying 'we have a "problem" at our company regarding management buy-in to operational risk management'. We all nodded our agreement until he said 'the problem we have is a good one, in that our businesses do too much risk management! Our businesses have just completed their 6,000th risk and control self assessment and we think they are doing too much.' This comment got the audience's attention. He then spent the rest of the talk outlining the reasons why they had achieved such a high level of 'embeddedness' including:

1. Never mention the 'C' word. C is for 'compliance'. What he meant was that you will never create buy-in by saying 'you must do this, you must to that'. The business needs to want to do it themselves. With that said, the role of Compliance is critical and the key to success with Compliance is to ensure that business understands the repercussions of not complying. That is, they understand the consequences of their actions.

2. Identify and deliver 'what's in it for them'. In the initial stages of developing the operational risk management function, it was identified that operational risk was costing each business dearly. Secondly management were remunerated partially

based on performance. Linking these two observations, operational risk management carried out a detailed analysis of each business. This included analysing the cost of each major type of operational risk, suggesting ways that could be used to reduce that risk and associated cost. A budget was set for each major risk cost and actual cost against budget was tracked and reported monthly. The risk team then approached the business under the label of 'business performance partner' and not 'operational risk management'. When this information was presented to the business and they were asked 'Is this something you would be interested in receiving regularly?' the only answer was yes. Only then was the department introduced as 'operational risk management'.

Case Study

On the first operational risk management 'awareness' training session at a new client I noticed that the head of the banking retail division arrived ten minutes late, sat at the back with his arms folded and focused his attention on his mobile phone. I thought to myself he is going to be a tough person to convince. I need to identify 'What's in it for him'. In my prior experience in retail banking, I had seen the common practice of monthly branch checklists being completed and consolidated for reporting purposes. So, during the 'Compliance' section of the presentation I asked the retail head, 'Do you do monthly branch checklists and how long do they take to collect and collate?, When do you receive the consolidated results and report to management?' The answers were 'Yes', '10 days', 'about 20 days after month end'. I had a sample checklist set up on the operational risk system and ran through the on-line process which included automatic follow up for non-completes, escalations for non-completes and negative answers and automatic preparation of the report. This process required little effort and the branch report could be produced within five days of month end. Having seen this, his body language changed to a forward lean, hands unfolded on the table, mobile phone in pocket and the question 'when can you come in and set this up for me?'

AN INTEGRATED APPROACH TO OPERATIONAL RISK MANAGEMENT

'Integrated' can be used to refer to many things including:

1. Integration of risk management into day-to-day operations. Embedding risk management into the organisation's day-to-day practices has been addressed earlier in this chapter.

2. Integration of the various components of operational risk management.

3. Integration across all operational risk disciplines.

INTEGRATION OF THE VARIOUS COMPONENTS OF OPERATIONAL RISK MANAGEMENT

Throughout this book, the key components of operational risk management have been addressed, being:

- risk and control self assessment and scenario analysis

- key risk indicators

- risk incident management and recording

- external and internal compliance

- treatment improvements

- quantification

- reporting.

In addition, internal audit, although not part of pure operational risk management, should ideally be included in any integrated system in order to maximise efficiencies and effectiveness.

What is an Integrated Systems Approach?

An integrated systems approach is illustrated at Figure 12.1 and involves:

1. Central registers which contain common data such as risk causes, risk events, risks effects, controls, compliance obligations and key risk indicators linking to, and feeding from, each risk management function.

2. Action tracking, reporting, workflow and internal audit applying and linking to all functions.

3. Linking between operational risk management functions in terms of sharing data and updating. Examples are:

   - Linking the **RCSA** process to **compliance** where controls selected and assessed in the RCSA are automatically shared with compliance for subsequent attestation;

- Linking **incident management** with **compliance** obligations to enable identification of specific compliance breaches;

- Linking **scenario analysis** with **RCSA** to enable identification of risks with potentially large consequences; and

- Linking **RCSA** with **incident management** to provide the user with a list of the controls that were linked to that incident risk type for consideration as to which of these controls may have failed to allow the incident to occur.

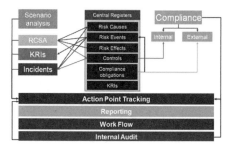

Figure 12.1   An integrated approach to operational risk management

The Benefits of an Integrated Systems Approach

In order to consider the benefits of an integrated systems approach to operational risk management it is first useful to consider the shortcomings of a non-integrated approach. Such an approach involves no common registers, separate systems and databases for each risk function, separate RCSA, KRI and incident management systems, separate and multiple treatment improvement registers and separate compliance systems. This non-integrated approach leads to:

1. Different naming conventions for the same risk (risk causes, risk events and risk effects) and controls in different business units and across different risk disciplines. This prevents risk aggregation and comparison.

2. The duplication or multiplication of the same information across multiple systems.

3. The inability to efficiently aggregate data from different systems for consolidated reporting purposes.

4. The inability to link data from different systems, preventing the collection of valuable insights into risk behaviour.

The key benefit of an integrated approach is in overcoming the above drawbacks by:

1. Maximising the use of a common language. For example, the same risk should have the same name, regardless of where in the organisation it exists.

2. Minimising the duplication of information.

3. Maximising the sharing of information and therefore efficiency of the risk process.

4. Facilitating the creation of integrated 'dashboard' reporting at the group and business unit level.

5. Allowing consolidated risk reporting across all of the operational risk components (RCSA, KRIs, incident management, compliance and action tracking) by risk type.

INTEGRATION ACROSS ALL RISK DISCIPLINES

As we have discussed earlier in this chapter, it is common that the risk specialist areas within an organisation will have developed their own methodologies and processes, developed or purchased their own risk software and have their own specific regulatory requirements and reporting needs. Put simply, they are often more advanced than the overall operational risk management discipline. However difficult it may be, integration of these functions under one 'Operational Risk Management' umbrella, as illustrated in Figure 12.2, has many advantages including:

- One common language and acronyms;

- One common methodology and framework, leading to a common way to look at all risk – this provides a greater understanding and awareness of risk by the business as they only have one framework to understand;

- The use, as far as possible, of one system;

- An increase in communication between the various specialist risk disciplines;

- Maximising the use of common information;

- Maximising the cross fertilisation of information between each risk discipline;

- The ability to aggregate and create consolidated risk information; and

- One risk face to the business, that is, all risk disciplines can approach the business under the one 'face' of operational risk management, rather than as separate disparate functions.

Figure 12.2   Integration of risk management across risk disciplines

HURDLES TO INTEGRATION

There are many hurdles to successful integration across risk disciplines. The most common seems to be resistance to change. Owners of specialist risk management areas, who have developed their department over many years, are quite understandably resistant to change when they see the required changes being only for the common good of the organisation as a whole, rather than any direct benefit to their own business area. Commonly we hear from these managers:

> *'Why change something that isn't broken?'*

> *'What's in it for us?'*

'We are different than the others. We have different objectives and focus.'

'We are more advanced than any other department and integration will drag us back.'

'We have separate requirements and regulations.'

'We have invested a lot of time and money in where we are today. Why should we change it?'

'What you are proposing to replace our current system with is not as good.'

'We need to be independent.'

Many of these comments are valid and they must be addressed and resolved in order for integration to be accepted. For example, it is usually valid that:

1. Certain risk disciplines will have slightly differing objectives and focus. This must be respected and recognised in any integration.

2. There may be different external requirements which have to be accommodated.

3. There may be different reporting needs, to both external and internal parties.

4. There may be a requirement for independence and therefore segregation may be required between the various risk disciplines.

5. Confidentiality of data will be essential for some risk areas.

Case Study

Purchase of, and migration to, a new integrated system. The client was a large national company with established risk disciplines. On introducing new operational risk management software to the business for the first time, it was clear that there would be strong resistance from certain areas. As a result, the approach taken was to:

- Roll out the new system to cover new risk functions not already covered by existing disciplines. This validated the system in management's eyes and gained a degree of acceptance.

- Review each specialist risk to assess what was currently being done. The new system was then assessed as to how it could not only provide the existing functionality but also provide improvements to what was currently being done.

- Gain an agreement with the specialist risk areas that a change to the system would only occur once it was proved that the new system was at least as good, if not better, than the legacy system(s).

- Parallel run the new system with the legacy systems until the specialist risk area WANTED to change to the new system.

This approach had great success as the specialist risk areas felt in control of any change.

CONCLUSION

Operational risk management, although practiced in one form or another since the beginning of time, is relatively young in its modern, more formalised form. This book has attempted to provide an introductory yet comprehensive look at operational risk as we head further into the twenty-first century. Operational risk management as a discipline is developing rapidly and I believe, becoming slowly accepted as an essential component of any organisation, however big or small. In order to gain wider acceptance and adoption, a greater awareness of operational risk and available management techniques is required. I hope to some degree that this book aids in that process.

Index

If you have found this book useful you may be interested in other titles from Gower

A Short Guide to Reputation Risk
Garry Honey
Paperback: 978-0-566-08995-4
e-book: 978-0-566-08996-1

A Short Guide to Fraud Risk:
Fraud Resistance and Detection
Martin Samociuk, Nigel Iyer, Edited by Helenne Doody
Paperback: 978-0-566-09231-2
e-book: 978-0-566-09232-9

A Short Guide to Ethical Risk
Carlo Patetta Rotta
Paperback: 978-0-566-09172-8
e-book: 978-0-566-09173-5

A Short Guide to Procurement Risk
Richard Russill
Paperback: 978-0-566-09218-3
e-book: 978-0-566-09219-0

GOWER

A Short Guide to Customs Risk
Catherine Truel
Paperback: 978-1-4094-0452-1
e-book: 978-1-4094-0453-8

A Short Guide to Political Risk
Robert McKellar
Paperback: 978-0-566-09160-5
e-book: 978-0-566-09161-2

A Short Guide to Equality Risk
Tony Morden
Paperback: 978-1-4094-0450-7
e-book: 978-1-4094-0451-4

A Short Guide to Facilitating Risk Management:
Engaging People to Identify, Own and Manage Risk
Penny Pullan and Ruth Murray-Webster
Paperback: 978-1-4094-0730-0
e-book: 978-1-4094-0731-7

Visit **www.gowerpublishing.com** and

- search the entire catalogue of Gower books in print
- order titles online at 10% discount
- take advantage of special offers
- sign up for our monthly e-mail update service
- download free sample chapters from all recent titles
- download or order our catalogue